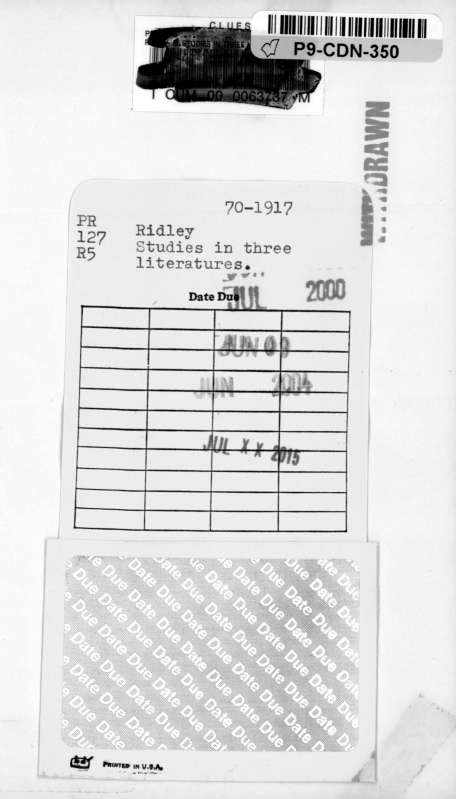

STUDIES IN THREE LITERATURES

STUDIES IN
THREE
LITERATURES

ENGLISH, LATIN, GREEK
CONTRASTS AND COMPARISONS

M. R. RIDLEY, M.A.

Lecturer at Bedford College, London
Formerly Fellow of Balliol College, Oxford

LONDON
J. M. DENT & SONS LTD

To J. E. L. R.
(pp. 103-4)

CONTENTS

PREFACE

DURING MANY YEARS OF TEACHING, BOTH IN CLASSICS AND IN English, I have become steadily more aware of the amount of pleasure missed by reading in watertight compartments, and the incalculable gain secured by 'comparative' reading. 'Compartmental' reading was enforced on many readers in their student days by the exacting demands of intensively specialized syllabuses, so that the student of the Classics had—or thought he had—'no time for' the reading of English, except as casual relaxation, while the student of English or French had equally no time to keep up his Latin and Greek, if any. But the habit of mind thus induced is apt to persist when there is no longer any need for it. Readers see literature as a number of separate fields, delimited by firmly erected fences; and, instead of demolishing the fences, they are apt, when they venture from one field into another, to close the gate carefully, if only half-consciously, behind them.

Thereby, I think, they lose much. The appreciation of the literature of one nation is greatly sharpened by an awareness of its differences from, or similarities to, the literature of others. The pleasure of reading *Paradise Lost* is made fuller if it is read alongside Homer and Virgil, and the pleasure of reading the *Aeneid* is enhanced if memories of the *Iliad* and *Paradise Lost* are floating in the reader's mind; some knowledge of the peculiarities of the Greek drama throws into prominence some peculiarities of the Elizabethan, and vice versa; a reading of Greek, Latin, and English lyrics not as belonging to mutually exclusive 'courses of study,' but in parallel, will not only lead to a more alert appreciation of the particular beauties of each kind, but also—and even more important—will illuminate the different national tempers which made the lyrics what they are.

This book is offered to those many readers who have less Greek and Latin than they would wish, in the hope that it may help them towards the rewards of such 'comparative reading.' I hope also that even readers who are well versed in the classical languages may find in it, among much that to them will be obvious and elementary, a few suggestions which will stimulate a keener enjoyment in the reading of our own English writers.

References are given to almost all passages. A peppering of footnotes is apt to be vexatious, but—as I know from baffled experience—not nearly so vexatious as wanting to look at a quoted passage in its context and not knowing where to find it. And no one is obliged to bother with a footnote which he does not need. The 'Oxford Books' of Greek, Latin, and English Verse are referred to by initials.

I have given translations of, I think, all quotations from Greek and Latin. To those who read these languages as easily as their own this may seem merely officious. They can neglect the renderings. For others the translations will, I hope, save them from losing the thread of the argument while they struggle with an unfamiliar language.

I should add a note about some of the translations. Those which are not otherwise attributed are my own. This is not in the least because I think that my attempts are 'better' than the well known ones; far from it; several of those in verse are, as poetry, manifestly and painfully inferior; but they also, I hope, exemplify more clearly the particular point which I was at the moment trying to make (the point, often, of the spare simplicity of the original). Anyone who cares to look at Shelley's rendering of the epitaph by Plato quoted on page 89 will see what I mean. Shelley's four lines are one of his loveliest pieces of work, but he makes them lovely by adornment and expansion. The whole of his second line elaborates into a metaphor a single plain Greek adverb, the 'new splendour' of his fourth line is not in the Greek, and he misses the telling repetition of the Greek word for 'shine.' But the way of the translator is very hard.[1] Aiming at the beautiful simplicity of the Greek he is apt to

---

[1] There is an admirable discourse on the translator's difficulties in Part II of the introduction to *The Oxford Book of Greek Verse in Translation*.

achieve in English a simplicity which is merely thin or even ugly. The rightness of the aim may perhaps serve as excuse for the faults in execution.

In the translations from Homer, and in one or two of those from Virgil, I have ventured on occasion to shorten, feeling that the omission of some stock epithets in Homer, or a characteristic Virgilian duplication, helped to secure the true total effect.

Much of the substance of the book formed the substance of lectures delivered at Oxford and in London. I have not been at pains to remove or modify, except in some small details, that idiom of the lecture-room which it is never easy, and perhaps by no means always desirable, to eradicate.

M. R. R.

ACKNOWLEDGEMENTS

The author's cordial thanks are offered to Mrs George Bambridge, Messrs Macmillan & Co. Ltd and Messrs Doubleday & Co. for permission to quote verses by Rudyard Kipling, the sources of which are footnoted in the text; also to the Society of Authors as the literary representative of the Estate of the late A. E. Housman, Messrs Jonathan Cape Ltd publishers of A. E. Housman's *Collected Poems* and Messrs Henry Holt and Co. for one poem and extracts from others footnoted in the text; also to the Clarendon Press for three stanzas from Bridges's *Elegy on a Lady*. Other minor illustrative quotations are attributed to their sources by footnotes.

CHAPTER ONE

THREE LANGUAGES

IS THERE ANY REAL MEANING IN THE PHRASE 'A GREAT LANGUAGE'? It is sometimes used to mean no more than 'a language in which great books have been written.' But it can, I think, be pinned down to a more precise meaning than that, and at any rate, since great books can hardly be written except in a language of certain qualities, one can try to determine what qualities a language must have to allow great books to be written in it, or, for that matter, great speeches made, so that, even in the loosest sense, one can call it a 'great' language.

In the first place, it must be both lucid and flexible. For any idea which the writer or speaker wishes to express, whether of the study, the forum, or the field, he must find ready to hand the means of exactly unambiguous expression. That is the bare minimum, without which a language fails to perform its primary function, the function of a bridge by which thought crosses the silence which separates one mind from another. Then, on the side of syntax, the order of construction should be a help rather than a hindrance to thought: the bridge must not be too steep in pitch nor too stony in surface. Further, in addition to this bare minimum of lucidity and flexibility, one may not unreasonably demand a capacity for beauty and dignity. The language should have certain qualities of mere sound, an aptness to fall naturally into music, into melodiously sonorous phrases and harmoniously rhythmed periods.

A language that satisfies these demands must be ranked high. But before the highest rank can be reached there is a further requirement to be satisfied, a complement of the first. A completely *lucid* language is sensitive to the *intellect*, plastic to the touch of an intellectual distinction, however fine. But to be fully 'great' a language must be no less sensitive to the *emotions*, plastic to every distinction of mood, capable of varying in the subtlest and exactest harmony with each rise or fall of emotion, so that it can be sublime without turgidity, simple without baldness, impassioned without dishevelment. And this flexibility in both spheres, this capacity both for nice distinctions of meaning and for delicate differentiation of tone and value, can hardly come except from an abundant vocabulary and a wealth of so-called synonyms. 'So-called,' since there is no such thing as an exact synonym, and the power of apprehending the shade of distinction between two words which for crude practical purposes 'mean the same' is one of the graces of literary appreciation. The trained reader, besides, is sensible of associations as well as of distinctions of meaning, and upon this sensibility the trained writer plays. The full development of this sensibility is one of the last and best fruits of long experience and it is the final mark of a great language that it is rich in such possibilities of distinction and association.

I

With this preamble of requirements proposed, and I hope accepted, may we turn to concrete examples, and examine three languages? And first, Latin. The word which rises most naturally in the mind to describe the outstanding quality of Latin is the word which the great nation who spoke it used for one of their own most highly rated Roman virtues, *gravitas*. The likeness which is always, I think, to be traced between the character of a nation and the character of its language is here unmistakable. Latin is a difficult language, intractable, with none of the softer graces, but always, and above all things, forcible, direct, and dignified. In its earlier days, or at any rate its earlier literary days, it is also crudely unkempt and uncouth, with a kind of vigorous rusticity.

The defects were inherent in the language, with whatever limited measure of success they were later concealed or transformed; and since the final verdict is likely to be one of praise, even if it is restricted praise, it is as well to examine the defects first.

The language, then, is naturally ponderous. It falls with unhappy readiness into the bristling hexameters of Ennius, like that famous line in which no caesura and one dactyl bear up as best they can against five overwhelming spondees and the petrifying hiss of all the serpents of Medusa.[1] And this characteristic ponderosity, modified though it may be, is never eradicated, and the masters of Latin wisely used it, to magnificent effect, instead of fighting against it. Catullus' experiments in hendecasyllabics are astonishingly graceful, but they are a tour de force in a literary form quite alien to the genius of the language. The discriminating sculptor does not select granite for a statuette of a dancing nymph. It is also this weighty solidity in the language which is largely responsible for the Latin elegiac's failure to remind one of the Greek, its frequent failure to take rank as poetry at all. Take as an example the first four lines of Catullus' lament over his brother's grave:

> Multas per gentes et multa per aequora vectus
> Advenio has miseras, frater, ad inferias,
> Ut te postremo donarem munere mortis
> Et mutam nequiquam alloquerer cinerem.[2]

No one, surely, can miss the grave power of those lines. Here Catullus is working with, not against, his language, and evokes the full grandeur of his great instrument. Also, for various reasons, particularly a metrical scheme in the pentameter which later purists regarded as inadmissible, the lines are, for Latin elegiacs, comparatively free in movement. But set against them Callimachus' famous epitaph on Heraclitus.

> εἶπέ τις, Ἡράκλειτε, τεὸν μόρον, ἐς δέ με δάκρυ
> ἤγαγεν, ἐμνήσθην δ᾽ ὁσσάκις ἀμφότεροι
> ἥλιον ἐν λέσχῃ κατεδύσαμεν. ἀλλὰ σὺ μέν που,
> ξεῖν᾽ Ἁλικαρνησεῦ, τετράπαλαι σποδιή.

[1] Sparsis hastis longis campus splendet et horret.
[2] 'Through the lands of many nations I have travelled, and over many seas, and now I stand, my brother, in sorrow by your tomb, to offer you in death my last of all gifts, and speak in vain to the ashes that cannot answer' (*Carmina*, 101, *O.B.L.V.* 100).

αἱ δὲ τεαὶ ζώουσιν ἀηδόνες, ᾗσιν ὁ πάντων
ἁρπακτὴρ Ἀΐδης οὐκ ἐπὶ χεῖρα βαλεῖ.[1]

The whole movement of the two passages is different. In the one the caesura justifies its name; it is the axe which cuts the pentameter into two halves which struggle to unite. In the other it is no more than a pebble which causes a ripple in the smooth-flowing stream. And one may guess, by the way, that it was an awareness of this quality in their language which led the Roman lyrists to modify the Sapphic metre as they did. A more technical examination suggests that this rather sullen weightiness of Latin is due in part to a preponderance of long vowels and frequent cumbrous assemblages of warring consonants.

But the gravest count in the indictment of Latin is that of clumsiness. It is apt to move with a stiff, inflexible, and graceless angularity, and only a very moderate success rewarded the attempts to conceal this under flowing draperies. And it is one of the two great masters of Latin prose who is, in his philosophic writings, the most damaging witness for the prosecution. Cicero had recast his reluctant material till he could use it for all the diverse purposes of his infinitely varied and immaculately polished oratory; but even he could not temper it to the uses of philosophy. The language served him well in the cloudy atmosphere of the law courts, to persuade a bemused juryman that black was certainly white, or that either was quite probably grey; but it failed him, and exposed its indigence, in the clear light of the Academy, where the issue was not the acquittal or condemnation of a criminal, but the discovery and establishment of a truth.

The vocabulary is gravely deficient, or at least one-sided and ill-balanced, nor are there any ready means of supplying gaps. The language is, as one would expect the Roman language to

---

[1] 'One told me, Heraclitus, of your death, and brought the tears to my eyes as I remembered how often the two of us saw the sun to his rest with our talking. But now, my guest from Halicarnassus, you are lying somewhere far away, age-cold ashes. But your nightingales live on, and on them Hades, that rapes all away, shall not lay his hand.' This is, for the moment, the plainest prose translation that I can devise; see later pp. 88 and 157, for verse translations (O.B.G.V. 513).

be, grimly practical, uncompromisingly concrete, with a rude poverty of the words of abstract thought. It is also about as elastic as cast-iron. There is no chance of constructing a new compound epithet, prefixing three prepositions to ἰέναι (to go) and so creating a new verb, or using the article and the infinitive as substitute for a non-existent or temporarily forgotten noun. The writer is either driven to take refuge in Greek, an open confession of weakness; or he resigns himself to periphrases which confuse thought; or he is reduced to mere ambiguities, to a kind of intellectual algebra by which an ordinary word is to be used for x or the unknown quantity; and the reader must please remember that the writer does not mean what he says. It is true that Latin is uniquely rich in the possession of two Protean words, whose meaning, as young ears grow weary of hearing, is determined by context, the *par nobile, ratio* and *res*. The activities of the two words are indeed manifold, and a judicious use of them has led wise men to mistake ignorance for Latinity. But there is a radical defect in a language which can only pursue flexibility along the by-paths of ambiguity.

Finally, the syntax is, at any rate in literary Latin, a definite hindrance to thought. One hopes that in ordinary life it was not too grave a solecism to put an essential word or two near the beginning of a sentence, as a kind of signpost for the way-worn and benighted traveller; otherwise conversation must have been Meredithianly exhausting. But literary Latin, with its curiously conventional order of words, is a difficult medium to think in, and it is a mystery how any man on a mere hearing understood certain Ciceronian sentences. In reading, a furtive glance at the end of the sentence clears matters up. But that is a scandalous practice, even in detective stories; and anyway in the audience we are bound by the rigour of the game; we cannot fall into sin if we would. And Cicero, starting out with an accusative and a subject, leads us through a relatival, a final, and a temporal clause into the slough of a parenthesis, where we abandon hope, wondering whether Balbus entertained Flaccus to supper, or sent him to Rome, or ordered him build a wall. We are finally startled to discover that the last word is *interfecit* (killed) and the relevance of the intermediate clauses to their drastic culmination is lost. It is to be supposed that from hard necessity the Romans, like the Germans, grew skilled in the

B

mental acrobatics which their syntax demanded, and learned to keep a whole sentence suspended with its attendant clauses till the last few words determined its meaning. But this effort does not make it easier for the writer to convey his meaning, still less for his reader to apprehend it.

Yet, burdened though it was with these not inconsiderable disadvantages, Latin became a great literary language. The masters of Latin literature not only had the insight to perceive in the virtues of their language, and even in some of its defects, the possibilities of permanent greatness; they had also the technical skill to embody their vision in their work. In prose the heavy words, under the cunning hand of Cicero, fell into those sonorous periods whose clash and rebound raise dust enough to blind keener eyes and deceive more fastidious tastes than those of Roman jurymen. Cicero showed also the wide variations of tone which lay within the compass of the language, using it for florid rhetoric, or trenchant narrative, or quiet discourse, with apparently equal ease and certainly with equally telling effect. It seems, indeed, that Latin was peculiarly adapted to history, rhetoric, and letter-writing; all three, one observes, eminently practical and matter-of-fact branches of literature. It is a sad pity that Caesar's account of his campaigns is little read except to fortify the lower forms of schools. For it is a model of how great events can be related, by the man who directed their course, with that dignified simplicity which is one of the marks of the classic temper. As a record of part of the life of a great man it is an *aere perennius* monument; as an example of the *summa ars* it is a literary triumph. This is one of the prerogatives of Latin, that it can say a plain thing plainly and yet with a dignity the more perfect for being so unconscious. It is, then, even for the modern world, the only language for memorial inscriptions.

And for another kind of historical writing the language served even better. Opinions have varied about Tacitus as a historian, some critics thinking him so biased that it is almost idle labour to try to disentangle fact from innuendo, though the critical pendulum has lately been swinging the other way, and he has been presented in, I think, much truer colours. But there have never been two opinions about his power over words to express concentrated thought. He has few rivals simply as a narrator, but he has no rival at all in the short phrase packed with meaning, or the devastating force of his sardonic, mordant comments. Take the famous *felix opportunitate mortis*.[1] A whole paragraph of comment compressed into three words. And how simple! But could any other language have so compressed it? Try it in Greek, or try it in our own. 'Happy in the chance of his death?'—hopeless. 'Happy in the hour of his death?'— ambiguous. 'Happy that his death fell when it did?'—better, but *felix* is more than 'happy,' the English misses part of the force of *opportunitas*, and takes six words to say what Latin says in one. Or take, perhaps the most famous of all, *omnium consensu capax imperii nisi imperasset*,[2] that despair of translators. Tacitus owed much to his language, first for offering him a pair of words which gave an echo without exact repetition, secondly for being tolerant of the ellipse to which much of the pungency is due. Of course one can give the *sense* of the phrase in English —'Everyone thought that he had the qualities necessary for the Principate (and would have gone on thinking so) if he had never been Princeps,' but all the salt has gone out of it. 'He would have gone down to history as a born ruler—if he had never ruled'; better, but too much a paraphrase. ' "A born ruler"; the universal verdict, if he had never ruled'; possible, and perhaps about as near as English can come to working the essential ellipse, but not much more than a pale shadow of the Latin. I suppose that what best illustrates the peculiar power of which Tacitus and the Latin language between them are capable is a comparison with Gibbon, who is nearer to Tacitus, in both temper and manner, than any other English historian.

As to the suitability of Latin for letter-writing and rhetoric I need only cite the letters of Cicero and Horace as examples of the one; the orations of Cicero and Satires of Juvenal as examples of the other. For Juvenal is the supreme example of the rhetorician in poetry, with all the rhetorician's virtues, and most of the rhetorician's failings. Sadly often his most carefully calculated and powerful effects are marred by the line too much. He is one of those workmen who 'striving to do better than well, do but confound their skill in covetousness,' because they have never come to the knowledge of the last refinement which the

---

[1] *Agricola*, xlv.   [2] *Histories*, I. xlix.

artist learns, the instinct for the moment when he must restrain his too eager fingers from the ruinous last touch. But still in Juvenal's smithy this iron language glowed white hot, when some occasion fanned his smouldering and savage indignation, and he found it malleable for the forging of those rhetorical harpoons which sink their barbs so deep in the memory. Here are two instances from many. The first is fine in itself, though oddly disproportionate to its trivial context:

> Nocte quidem, sed luna videt, sed sidera testes
> Intendunt oculos.[1]

There is a frugality about it which is in the best Roman manner. Or take the two great lines which show Juvenal at his noblest, expressing the ideals of the old Roman character in those days of the great Republic upon which the decadent monarchy turned back its bloodshot eyes:

> Summum crede nefas animam praeferre pudori,
> Et propter vitam vivendi perdere causas.[2]

But the genius of the language did not set towards great poetry. Ennius, along with much intolerable stuff, struck out a line or two not unworthy of the sovereign city that was no huckster in war but a warrior.[3] Lucretius carried the development further and was the first to show some realization of the capabilities of his metre. He is hampered by his subject, the chariot wheels drive heavily, and at its best the verse is more remarkable for weight than beauty. But when, as once or twice, the emotional tension is high, and difficulties of scientific terminology are dismissed, there is in his tones a sombre dignity, the measured solemnity of great bells tolling, that no writer and no language have surpassed:

---

[1] Satire viii. 149–50. 'It was night indeed, but the moon was watching and the stars bent down their eyes to witness the deed.' But the 'deed' was nothing more heinous than the undignified behaviour of a man of consular rank who behaved like a gay young spark and drove a curricle through the streets.

[2] Satire viii. 83, 4. 'Count it the blackest sin to set life above honour, and for the sake of life to lose all that makes life worth living.'

[3] 'Non cauponantes bellum sed belligerantes.'

jam jam non domus accipiet te laeta, neque uxor
optima, nec dulces occurrent oscula nati
praeripere, et tacita pectus dulcedine tangent.[1]

or

quid sit amari
tanto opere, ad somnum si res redit atque quietem,
cur quisquam aeterno possit tabescere luctu.[2]

And yet the admiration which even Lucretius' achievement
provokes is an admiration half reluctant. We are uneasily
conscious of the difficulties overcome. *Tantae molis erat Romanam
condere Musam.*[3] Lucretius never learned that master-spell which
comes with an ease apparently so effortless from the lips which
Apollo has touched.

There was indeed only one Roman poet who learned it.
Virgil alone of his race raised Latin to the rank of a great
poetic language, and even he not completely. But under his
hands the hexameter takes on a subtler and mellower harmony.
It is true that he also shared in the easier triumphs of rhetoric,
and it is to him that we owe one of the finest of patriotic
exhortations:

tu regere imperio populos, Romane, memento;
(hae tibi erunt artes); pacisque imponere morem,
parcere subiectis et debellare superbos.[4]

But the writer of those lines is Virgil the Roman, Virgil the
deliberate and limited patriot. When we encounter Virgil the
universal poet, Virgil the wizard, he rises far above this, and
carries the language with him to the heights. There will be more
to say of Virgil later when we come to the epic, so for the moment
I will do no more than remind you of the sovereign spells:

[1] Lucretius, *De Rerum Natura*, iii. 894–6. 'Now never again shall
your home give you a happy welcome, nor your noble wife, nor shall
the sons you love race each other to win the first kiss, and touch your
heart with joy too deep for words.'

[2] *Ibid.* 909–11. 'What is there so bitter, if all returns to sleep and
peace at the last, to make any man pine away with age-long grief?'

[3] *Aeneid*, i. 33 (with *gentem* for 'Musam'). 'So huge a task it was
to found the Roman race.'

[4] *Aeneid* vi. 851–3. 'For you, O Roman, remember to hold the
nations of the world under your rule (these shall be your "arts"),
to enforce the ways of peace, to spare the conquered and war
down the proud.'

tendebantque manus ripae ulterioris amore[1]

olli dura quies oculos et ferreus urget
somnus, in aeternam clauduntur lumina noctem[2]

et dulces moriens reminiscitur Argos[3]

There are some who disparage Virgil as an unoriginal plagiarist. There is, they tell us, nothing new in him. They are looking for the essence of poetry in the wrong place, in the letter, not in the spirit. Perhaps there is nothing new in him—except himself; but that self might be enough to satisfy the most exacting seeker after novelty. And in any case novelty is not, or should not be, the first thing we demand of a poet; and it is at least true of Virgil and his Roman language that in all literature that unembittered melancholy, that temperate hope, and that sorrowful majesty of cadence, have been heard once only.

And whatever charges may be brought against Latin, and they are grave enough, of cacophony, clumsiness, and heaviness, there stands the fact that it was the language of several great writers and of at least one great poet. And at the very least it was the speech of the rulers of the world, a people with a surpassing genius for affairs, for government, jurisdiction, and war; and the stamp of their greatness is on the language which they spoke. If Latin was indeed no dialect of the philosophers, it was the speech of the nation of kings.

2

When we turn to Greek we step into a different world. We are engaged now with the language of a vivid and versatile nation, who took all life and all thought for their province, with a passion for beauty, and a never-satisfied hunger after truth. I suppose that the first quality in the language to fix the attention of the reader is the extraordinary beauty of mere sound. There are, no doubt, individual lines, but I doubt whether there are any sustained passages, in Virgil, which even to a sensitive ear

[1] *Aeneid* vi. 314. 'They kept stretching out their hands in longing for the farther shore.'

[2] *Aeneid* x. 745, 6. 'The iron sleep of death pressed down upon him, and his eyes closed into eternal night.'

[3] *Aeneid* x. 782. 'He died remembering the Argos that he loved.'

would bring pleasure of sound apart from meaning. But there
are plenty of people quite without Greek who take a keen
delight in the roll of the Homeric hexameter and in the more
delicate dance of the elegiac. Nor need this surprise us when we
recall those miracles of single words in which the language is so
rich, ῥοδοδάκτυλος, ἰοχέαιρα, ἐρατεινή. Or for a complete
passage take those famous four lines of Alcman, in the continuous
dactyls of which you can hear the murmuring of the Hybla bees,
and feel the gentle swell of the sea over which the ceryl flies.

> οὔ μ' ἔτι, παρθενικαὶ μελιγάρυες ἱμερόφωνοι,
> γυῖα φέρειν δύναται. βάλε δὴ βάλε κηρύλος εἴην,
> ὅς τ' ἐπὶ κύματος ἄνθος ἅμ' ἀλκυόνεσσι ποτῆται
> νηλεγὲς ἦτορ ἔχων, ἀλιπόρφυρος εἴαρος ὄρνις.[1]

If the language is beautiful, it is also infinitely flexible. In
Latin you can only say what the language will let you; in Greek
you can say what you like. The vocabulary is superabundant,
the syntax licenses all possible and some apparently impossible
constructions. For various reasons, in particular its wealth of
particles, there is a delicacy and finesse about the language
which no other language can even approach. It is the speech of
brilliant and subtle conversationalists. The Roman says *enim* or
autem or *immo vero* and the words shout at you like a sergeant-
major with the awkward squad; but the Greek insinuates an
apparently casual and innocent γὲ or πού, and the whole
value of the sentence is changed. There is something singularly
exhilarating and piquant about a language which can imply a
whole unexpressed sentence in the word γάρ. It is the very
language of the intellectual fencing school, keen and strong and
supple. And as the medium of thought Greek is the master
language. Of itself it stimulates clear thinking. The order of the
words in good Greek is the order of logic, and—a still more
valuable quality—it is possible to talk philosophy and yet slip
from one's shoulders the burden of a technical phraseology.

[1] *O.B.G.V.* 115
'No more, O musical maidens with voices ravishing-sweet!
    My limbs fail:—Ah that I were but a ceryl borne on the wing
Over the bloom of the wave amid fair young halcyons fleet,
    With a careless heart untroubled, the sea-blue bird of the spring!'
                                                    (W. Headlam)

Hence one is not deluded into confusing recognition of a phrase with exact comprehension of its meaning. In English the ground is all cluttered up with technical jargon, objective, subjective, essential and secondary qualities, idealism, realism, pragmatism, monism, dualism, and so on. When the philosophic contest grows hot, and the combatants seize these missiles, and the air is thick with hurtling and not too well directed -isms, the ordinary man may be forgiven if he is bewildered and thinks that the philosophic arena is no place for him. But αὐτὸ καθ' αὐτὸ and ἕκαστον ὅτι ἔστιν[1] are the language of ordinary men, and there is no escaping them. We may or may not agree with Plato; but at least there is no ambiguity about the exact subject in dispute.

If for thought Greek is immeasurably superior to Latin, for oratory it is probably inferior. For straightforward argument it can, of course, hardly be bettered, but for the more impassioned passages it is too volatile and tends to become dishevelled. But here one must go warily. The business of an orator is, after all, to persuade; and to persuade his immediate audience; and that audience therefore an audience of his countrymen. Hence of all forms of literature oratory is the most narrowly national, and hence of all forms the hardest to criticize. It so happens that we are by temperament nearer to the Romans than to the Athenians, and Cicero's qualities as an orator are apt to seem to us more satisfying than those of Demosthenes.

But whatever we may think of Greek as a vehicle for oratory, as regards the power of the ordinary 'bare word' the dialogues of Plato are in Greek and there is an end of it. Plato found ready to his hand unique material and he made unparalleled use of it. In no mode is he less than himself; from closely reasoned argument to the most delicate humour, from immortal single phrases to the sustained poetic inspiration of the great myths, everywhere he moves with unassertive mastery, and his language never fails him. It is precisely this adaptability—not at all peculiar to Plato—which makes it hard to criticize the language. Whatever is on hand to be said, and in whatever tone, the language has an exact appropriateness. One is perhaps tempted to single out the power, in which Homer is pre-eminent, of putting things in words so simple that they are

[1] The 'thing in itself' and 'each thing what it is.'

only saved from bathos by their poignancy.[1] But then one recalls that with equal ease the language can express the chiselled artistries of Sophocles, the vaguer and more grandiloquent sublimities of Aeschylus, or the rich comedy of Aristophanes. It is even long-suffering enough not to protest too loudly against the occasional maltreatment of Thucydides' 'speeches.'

Yet with all its manifold graces Greek comes short of Latin in one respect. It never, I think, moves with that massive dignity which marks the utterance of the dominant race. One may readily agree that there are 'greater' things in Sophocles alone than in the whole range of Latin literature, and yet believe that there is nothing at all in Greek which can in its own limited sphere approach the level of the last eight lines of the Regulus ode.

> Atqui sciebat quae sibi barbarus
> Tortor pararet, non aliter tamen
>   Dimovit obstantes propinquos,
>   Et populum reditus morantem,
>
> Quam si clientum longa negotia
> Diiudicata lite relinqueret,
>   Tendens Venafranos in agros,
>   Aut Lacedaemonium Tarentum.[2]

[1] Take, for example, Andromache directing preparations for Hector's return:

κέκλετο δ' ἀμφιπόλοισιν ἐϋπλοκάμοις κατὰ δῶμα
ἀμφὶ πυρὶ στῆσαι τρίποδα μέγαν, ὄφρα πέλοιτο
Ἕκτορι θερμὰ λοετρὰ μάχης ἐκ νοστήσαντι—
νηπίη, οὐδ' ἐνόησεν ὅ μιν μάλα τῆλε λοετρῶν
χερσὶν Ἀχιλλῆος δάμασε γλαυκῶπις Ἀθήνη

(Iliad, xxii. 442–6)

('And she called to the handmaidens to set a great cauldron over the fire, that there might be water hot for Hector's bathing when he came home from battle—she did not know, poor lady, that far from all bathing Athene had brought him low by the hands of Achilles.')

[2] Horace, Odes, iii. 5 (O.B.L.V. 141)

> 'Well witting what the torturer's art
> Designed him, with like unconcern
> The press of kin he push'd apart
> And crowds encumbering his return,

[continued

You remember how Stevenson wished that some Roman, Martial for choice, could return from the grave and show us by what conduct of the voice those thundering verses should be uttered. 'Thundering'; there you have it: Greek is too much i' the sun, its thunder too often that of Salmoneus. Hence arises the doubt which checks one in the act of setting Greek above all languages. Is there a fatal facility about this lovely tongue? Is it too εὐτράπελος (facilely versatile), like the men who spoke it? Even in Plato a hypercritical mood may find a trace of weakness, a hint of

> jellies soother than the creamy curd.

Is there too smooth a fluency? There are certainly few tonic discords. For the value of such discords I need only recall that passage in which an English critic with an infallible ear for the ring of words analysed a famous sentence of one of the greatest of his forerunners, the great Miltonic sentence on virtue.[1] Also, Greek is too lenient to the inferior workman. Both Latin and English demand a craftsman to handle them; both remorselessly betray shoddy work. But in Greek, whether prose or poetry, it sometimes seems to matter little what you say, and almost less how you say it; the language has so rare a beauty of its own that it conceals inferiority of workmanship or triviality of thought behind that 'golden opalescent haze' of which we used to hear.

But it must seem a railing accusation which can find no graver charge than excess of beauty and fluency. The charge is indeed a real one and deserves consideration; but, when all is said, Greek is still the language in which were written some of those passages before which criticism grows wisely silent, whose power and perfection make comment an insult and even praise an impertinence. A language which can claim the farewell of Hector and Andromache, the Cassandra scene of the *Agamemnon*,

---

[1] R. L. Stevenson, *The Art of Writing*, chapter I, 'On some technical elements of style in Literature.'

> As though, some tedious business o'er
> Of clients' court, his journey lay
> Towards Venafrum's grassy floor,
> Or Sparta-built Tarentum's bay.'
>   (Conington)

the *Oedipus Tyrannus*, and the Myth of Er, can stand at the bar
of any tribunal without much fear of the verdict.

3

When the third goddess presents herself for judgement, Paris is
embarrassed by his familiarity with her, which both helps and
hinders a just decision. On the one hand we are free from a
disability which hampers all study of the Classic languages.
With them, the mere fact that we must always read the written,
and can never hear the spoken, word is at once a more serious
and a more blankly insuperable obstacle than we always realize
or are ready to admit. No study however close, joined to
sympathy and insight however keen, can compensate for the
lack of living conversation. It is only by the unconscious
practice of daily and hourly use that the ear and the mind learn
gradually the precise value of words, which are appropriate and
which inadvisable in which contexts. Such a delicate literary
sixth sense we can hardly hope to acquire with the Classic
languages. What, for example, was the distinction between
ὄνειρος and ὄνειρον except the scansion of their plurals?
How far are the letters of Caelius Rufus in the aristocratic slang
of the day? What would have represented to a Greek the relation between the legitimate 'begin' and the supposedly
unpardonable 'commence?' Was there anything to correspond
to the worst abominations of the lesser English Augustans,
'noble steed,' 'generous ire' and the rest of those misbegotten
frigidities? What, for the matter of that, would have represented
the difference between 'steed' and 'horse?' What should one
have said to cause the cultivated Athenian the kind of shudder
which affects the cultivated Englishman at the lines

> And then uprose the great Montrose
> In the middle of the room.[1]

In another important respect, however, we are less well situa-
ted for examining our own language. It is too much with us. Latin
and Greek are 'dead,' not in the sense which makes the modern
world so foolishly eager to erect a tombstone, saying 'And,
thank God, buried,' but in the sense that their development has

[1] Aytoun, *Lays of the Scottish Cavaliers*.

ceased; we have for our dissection the complete and preserved organism. English is still growing, and our examination of the older structures is perhaps prejudiced because we are unconsciously aware, and not consciously enough observant, of the sequence which relates them to the newer developments of our own time. But our nearness need not be allowed to distort our perspective and we can make at least an attempt to adjudicate on the claim of English to rival Latin and Greek.

In mere beauty of sound English can hardly make any pretensions as against Greek; nor does it of itself possess that weight and dignity which seem to belong as a prerogative to the most casual assemblage of Latin words.[1] This will be the less

---

[1] It may be interesting in connection with this question of sound to compare three descriptions of which the second and third are clearly derived from the first:

ἀπέβη γλαυκῶπις Ἀθήνη
Οὔλυμπόνδ’, ὅθι φασὶ θεῶν ἕδος ἀσφαλὲς αἰεὶ
ἔμμεναι· οὔτ’ ἀνέμοισι τινάσσεται οὔτε ποτ’ ὄμβρῳ
δεύεται οὔτε χιὼν ἐπιπίλναται, ἀλλὰ μάλ’ αἴθρη
πέπταται ἀνέφελος, λευκὴ δ’ ἐπιδέδρομεν αἴγλη.

Odyssey, vi. 41–5.

('Grey-eyed Athene went away to Olympus, where, they say, is for ever the secure dwelling of the immortals; it is never shaken by winds or wetted by rain, nor does snow ever fall there, but a cloudless heaven, exceeding clear, is spread above it, and a bright sheen is over all.')

apparet divum numen sedesque quietae
quas neque concutiunt venti nec nubila nimbis
aspergunt neque nix acri concreta pruina
cana cadens violat semperque innubilus aether
integit, et large diffuso lumine rident.

Lucretius, *D.R.N.*, iii. 18–22

('There appears the majesty of the immortals and their peaceful dwellings, which no winds shake or clouds sprinkle with rain, nor does snow spoil their beauty, falling white and congealed by bitter frost, but an ever-cloudless heaven is over them and they smile in a radiance that is spread over all.')

To the island valley of Avilion,
Where falls not hail, or rain, or any snow,
Nor ever wind blows loudly; but it lies
Deep-meadow’d, happy, fair with orchard-lawns
And bowery hollows crown’d with summer sea.

(Tennyson, *Morte d’Arthur*)

surprising when on examining any page of English writing we find a broadcast profusion of consonants, a scant admixture of vowels, and of that admixture many short and of an indeterminate sound. Is there any aesthetic crime beyond the capacity of a language which has to admit the ownership of so grotesque a monosyllable as the word 'strength,' seven consonants, representing at least five full consonantal sounds, and submerged beneath them one panting little vowel? It is no wonder that in bad writers we find 'cacophony supreme, the rattle of incongruous consonants only relieved by the jaw-breaking hiatus, and whole phrases not to be articulated by the powers of man.' But in this very nature, exacting and difficult, English shares with Latin one advantage over Greek. The workshop of English letters is an unwelcoming place for the incompetent or idle craftsman. The apprenticeship is hard, as those who have experienced it tell us, the occasions of despair many, the final successes rare and hardly won. The workman is not dealing with plastic clay in which almost the act of thought moulds Galatean statues; his material is blocks and chips of unwrought stone, spread before him in a bewildering profuseness. He has to build without mortar, as men in the northern counties their walls, by apt fitting of piece to piece. But the structure, if skilfully built, has a close-knit and compact strength; it is dangerously superfluous to add, and mere ruin to remove or alter.

And the English writer, no less than the English speaker, is perpetually faced by a further difficulty inherent in this inhospitable tongue. It shares with other uninflected languages a lamentable proneness to rush into ambiguities. A divorce, for instance, between relative and antecedent is perilous; but too strict an insistence on their union often does no more than strain the relation between other members of the sentence. Here no doubt is the difficulty which leads writers of the staccato school to seek a precarious safety in a style of such uncivil abruptness, reminding one of the spasms which attend the sudden starting of a goods train.

But English has two prime advantages. Whereas Greek and Latin were thoroughbred, English is hybrid and shows the advantages of cross-breeding. And whereas Greek seems to emerge full grown, and Latin was too artifically trained on foreign models, English reached the main climax of its development under the hands of men of genius, working with both native and imported elements, in an age of springing vitality.

The English writer draws upon a vocabulary of incomparable richness, strength and delicacy, which has inherited the wealth of both Saxon and Romance languages. And it is a commonplace no less important than trite that since one of these was the tongue of the serf and the other of his lord, the one of the country and the other of the court, we have for many things two words, the one homely and direct, of the soil, the other ornate and stately, of the palace. To which is sometimes to be added a third, since of the words of Latin origin some came over with the monks and some in a foreign dress with the Conqueror. This richness is full of pitfalls which trap the steps of the unwary. Some writers, mistaking length for strength, and the cult of the abstract for culture, load their periods with Latin polysyllables. They are afraid of the power of the short and racy Saxon, which they dare not use, which is indeed a kittle tool in the hands of the unskilled, mainly because if a writer uses short concrete words he is obliged to think. On the other side are reactionaries who are for confining language to what they like to call 'the sabre-cuts of Saxon speech,' though it is hard to see why a man armed with two weapons, each perfect in its kind, should wilfully throw one of them away. A sabre is an admirable weapon in the right place at the right time, but there are times and places in which a rapier, or even a stiletto, will be less conspicuous and more effective. And it is the peculiar strength of English that it can combine two modes of expression, neither in itself complete, so that each supplies the deficiencies of the other and their contrast gives added strength to both. Consider the effects produced in the Book of Common Prayer by the reiterated pairs of synonyms, 'dissemble nor cloke,' 'assemble and meet,' 'erred and strayed.' And it is interesting to notice the effects which a skilful writer achieves by the use of the difference in tone between the two classes of words. The master touch in one of Wordsworth's lyrics is the clash in the last two lines between the Romance word 'diurnal' and the homely Saxon monosyllables which surround it.

In the second place English is a manufactured language. The Elizabethans took their native speech as the development of five hundred years had given it them; they found it still plastic; they shaped and moulded it. They experimented in rhythms and metres and syntax and figures of speech. They perpetrated frequent absurdities and committed some crimes. The Classical metres were a Procrustean bed from which the torturers released such mis-shapen and halting deformities as one would think confidently never to see again were it not that modern fingers still sometimes reach after the old levers. Euphuism, too, and the Elizabethan 'conceit' were often no better than a debasement of both language and thought. But it is fair to remember that the Elizabethans lived in an age when all fields of human activity were open to the free-lance and explorer. All the writers were 'makers'; there is no trace here of the slow sleeping-sickness of Alexandrianism. And no doubt with the rest of their making they made, like other great men, great mistakes. But even these they made with a full-blooded magnanimity which is more fertile than pettifogging accuracy. We need not too rigorously censure their blunders; and to themselves we owe it to recall what they made of their language and ours, an instrument of many stops and pipes, before which the inferior artist stands as impotently as the two courtiers before Hamlet, but from which the fingers of a master can elicit melodies of a lovelier purity and harmonies of a richer splendour than are within the compass of any other language of men. Consider that within little more than half a century were produced those two bodies of work so diverse in spirit and manner, alike only in greatness, the plays and poems of Shakespeare, the poems and prose writings of Milton. And, if this were not enough, there is the English Bible. One could quote without end from the first two to illustrate the infinite variety of English—she is indeed the Cleopatra among languages—remembering the songs of Ariel and the ravings of Lear, *Paradise Lost* and *L'Allegro*. But all the proof that is needed is contained in the pages of the book which from the literary point of view is the most wonderful anthology in the world, that collection of myth, epic, history, lyric, mysticism, idyll, and letter-writing which we call the Authorised Version of the English Bible. It is the most precious literary possession of any European nation. It lies behind all our religion, and all our greatest literature. In it we see the simplicity and dignity which mark the 'Classic' languages, but through the simplest statement one's ear may often catch a strange and deeper undertone; and it rises no less than they to the heights of grandeur, but on more certain wings, in a kind of exultant triumph. Consider the sentence which one who was himself a master of letters described as the crashing overture to a great drama: 'Belshazzar the king made a great feast to a thousand of his lords, and drank wine before the thousand.'[1] On analysis, how little there is in it, a few quite ordinary words, mostly monosyllables. And yet, what a sentence! Or again, for the other note, the thirty-two-foot stop: 'Who is this that cometh from Edom, with dyed garments from Bozrah? this that is glorious in his apparel, travelling in the greatness of his strength?'[2] There is something about this, a hidden fire at the heart of the gem, which is beyond almost anything that Greece and Rome can offer. Take for further illustration two longer passages, one at the height of poetic inspiration, the other plain unadorned narrative, the Bunyan style.

'Arise, shine; for thy light is come, and the glory of the Lord is risen upon thee. For, behold, the darkness shall cover the earth, and gross darkness the people: but the Lord shall arise upon thee, and his glory shall be seen upon thee. And the Gentiles shall come to thy light, and kings to the brightness of thy rising . . . . The sun shall be no more thy light by day; neither for brightness shall the moon give light unto thee: but the Lord shall be unto thee an everlasting light, and thy God thy glory. Thy sun shall no more go down; neither shall thy moon withdraw itself: for the Lord shall be thine everlasting light, and the days of thy mourning shall be ended.'[3]

'But when the fourteenth night was come, as we were driven up and down in Adria, about midnight the shipmen deemed that they drew near to some country; and sounded, and found it twenty fathoms: and when they had gone a little farther, they sounded again, and found it fifteen fathoms. Then fearing lest we should have fallen upon rocks, they cast four anchors out of the stern, and wished for the day.'[4]

There is no time, and I think no need, to quote further for the range of English. I will do no more than recall a few familiar passages; the war in Heaven; the autumn leaves in Vallombrosa;

---

[1] Daniel v. 1.
[2] Isaiah lxiii. 1.
[3] Isaiah lx. 1–3, 19, 20.
[4] Acts xxvii. 27–9.

the last two lines of *Paradise Lost*; Macbeth's epitaph on Duncan; Cleopatra's last speech; the song for Fidele; the *Ode to a Nightingale* and *Kubla Khan*, which between them hold all the distilled sorceries of 'Romanticism'; the 'Conversation' between Hannibal and Marcellus, and the *Epitaph on an Army of Mercenaries*, both fine-drawn, *limatus*, tense with the strained classic reserve; *Levana and Our Ladies of Sorrow*; the magical strong music of *Deirdre of the Sorrows*.

Remembering these and other like passages, need one be afraid of making a judgement which sets our own language above those of Greece and Rome? The commonwealth of letters is cosmopolitan in the best sense of a term that has fallen on evil days; and in that commonwealth there is no place for the vulgar patriotism which is ignobly born of ignorance and prejudice; nor must one forget that the wealth of English is in large part just its inheritance from Greek and Latin. But I believe that English at its highest, while it falls somewhat short of the one for inevitable dignity, and of the other for inevitable beauty, can yet match Latin for power and Greek for charm; and has besides some indefinable spell to which the other two were strangers. If English has neither the *gravitas* of Regulus nor the sunshine loveliness of Helen, she is like the dark queen to whom the gods had not been lavish of mere beauty, who took the hearts of men captive in her 'strong toil of grace.'

CHAPTER TWO

PRIMITIVE EPIC

HAVING NOW EXAMINED BRIEFLY CERTAIN GENERAL DIFFERENCES between the three languages, let us become more specific, and consider them as vehicles for different literary forms. And let us begin our examination with the Epic.

In the first place, then, what is Epic? One can evade the difficulty lazily by saying that Epic is the *Iliad*, the *Odyssey*, the *Aeneid*, *Beowulf*, the *Lusiads*, the *Song of Roland*, *Paradise Lost*, *Sigurd*, leaving the reader to work out for himself the common qualities in these diverse works which have induced the judgement of the world to affix to them a common label. Or one can go to the first-aid station of the distressed literary critic, the fountain-head of literary criticism, Aristotle. Aristotle, however, is less helpful than usual, though not less dry. Epic, he tells us, is a narrative form of representation in metre; its plot ought to be concerned with one complete action, having beginning, middle, and end; its kinds are the same as those of tragedy; it can be ἁπλῆ (simple) or πεπλεγμένη (complex[1]), and ἠθική (primarily concerned with character) or παθητική (primarily concerned with the sufferings of the participants). (The *Iliad* is ἁπλῆ and παθητική, the *Odyssey* πεπλεγμένη and ἠθική.) It must be of such a length that one can get a bird's eye view of beginning and end. There must be variety, to produce a change of mood in the hearers, since monotony very soon produces satiety, and ruins an epic.

[1] Not a satisfactory translation, though the accepted one. By πεπλεγμένη Aristotle does not mean 'containing various interwoven threads (sub-plots and so on)', but 'containing "recognition" or "discovery" and "reversal of fortune".'

Experience has decided that the hexameter is the only metre. Epic will permit much grosser improbabilities than tragedy, since you do not see them, you only hear them. Homer, in particular, taught all other epic writers ψευδῆ λέγειν ὡς δεῖ[1].

Now all this exhibits Aristotle's usual acumen. But to us it is only partially helpful; for if you will consider again the list of epics with which we began, you will find that there are differences between them with which Aristotle makes no reckoning, and differences which to us are more important than any which he suggests. One needs no definition or minute analysis of impression to be aware that the *Iliad*, the *Odyssey* and *Beowulf* are one thing, the *Aeneid* and *Paradise Lost* quite another thing. The first three have a similar emotional appeal. They stir the imagination by the same technique; and though *Paradise Lost* and the *Aeneid* have many mutual differences they are yet in technique and appeal far nearer to one another than either is to the other three. It was no fault of Aristotle's that he failed to reckon with the difference between the two groups, since he had never met an example of the second; and wherein exactly the difference lies we will consider later. For the moment it is enough that to the ordinary reader the difference is apparent. And it has been generally agreed to affix to the one type of epic the label 'primitive,' and to the other the label 'literary.' These two labels do not imply any comparison of value between the two types. Another term sometimes used, 'authentic' epic, begs the question, and does imply such comparison, since it implies as its correlative the derogatory term 'spurious.' For the moment, therefore, the less we confuse the issue by using the term 'authentic' the better, though I shall return to it later.

Let us confine our attention for the present to the primitive epic, examining its aims, and the methods by which it attempts to achieve them. The sole object of the primitive epic is to *tell a story*; just that. The story may be of events, historic or semi-historic, like the *Iliad* or the *Song of Roland*; or of straightforward adventure and fairy story mingled, like the *Odyssey*. But the aim is identical, to tell this story as vividly and movingly

[1] Literally 'to tell lies in the right way,' but in fact the phrase has a wider scope: 'how to present a fallacy so that the reader himself, by false reasoning, accepts it as fact.'

as it can be told; to transport the hearer into the world of the story, so that he does not watch the action as in a picture, but joins in it as in life. He is to be bitterly anxious about the fate of the actors, to share their triumphs and their woes, to weep with them, and, less often, to laugh with them. The actors may be, and usually are, high-born and heroic, kings and the sons and daughters of kings, if not gods and the sons and daughters of gods. (The primitive epic is, indeed, apparently very snobbish in its sympathies.) But the important thing about them is neither their rank nor their divinity, but the humanity they share with us, the fact that they are men and women of like passions with ourselves, working out their salvation or destruction on the same stage as we, living the same life, and meeting in the end the same death. What does it matter that Nausicaa is a king's daughter? She is a girl playing with her companions, a type of eternal maidenhood. What does it matter, when we sit in the hut watching Achilles' agony over Patroclus, that his father is a king and his mother a goddess? He is a man weeping for his friend. The primitive epic, in short, has no object but to tell a great story with such power that the hearers sit spellbound in the shadowy hall. In spite of Lascelles Abercrombie, and the views so well expressed in his stimulating and very provocative book on the epic,[1] the primitive epic has, I believe, no ulterior object of showing us man's fate in a glass darkly, or of symbolizing anything at all. Its object is to enthral the heart, not to provoke the intellect.

Now what difficulties has the composer of primitive epic to face, and how does he meet them? I spoke a moment ago of the hearers. This word gives the key to many qualities of primitive epic, and suggests the opportunities, no less than the difficulties, of the composer. This epic is to be recited to an audience, not read by an individual. In the first place then, the unhappy reciter—rhapsode, jongleur, skald—must get his audience reduced to some sort of order. This was evidently not always easy. Lascelles Abercrombie gave so admirable an illustration of this difficulty that it would be both affectation and waste of time to look for a better. In the *Chanson d'Antioche* the first section opens:

[1] The Epic: Lascelles Abercrombie; Martin Secker (The Art and Craft of Letter Series).

> Seigneurs, faites silence; et que tout bruit cesse,
> Si vous voulez entendre une glorieuse chanson.
> Aucun jongleur ne vous en dira une meilleure.

(The reciter, you will observe, cannot afford to be modest about either his own attainments or the quality of his epic merchandise.) After this he makes a kind of false start, which might no doubt develop into a true one if the circumstances were favourable. Clearly, however, they were not, and the audience was too much occupied by its own disputes to attend, for the second section begins:

> Barons, écoutez-moi, et cessez vos querelles!
> Je vous dirai une très-belle chanson.

And after some further tuning of the instruments the section ends:

> Ici commence la chanson où il y a tant à apprendre.

But does the très belle chanson begin? Not a bit of it. There is indeed a kind of introduction, but it demanded, and probably received, no more attention than the incidental music before the modern play. And clearly the audibility was still low, since the fourth section beings:

> Maintenant (there is a pathetic appeal in the word)
> maintenant, seigneurs, écoutez ce que dit l'Écriture.

But not even l'Écriture can command silence. As the fifth section opens it appears that there was a lull, which gave the jongleur a chance, though he is careful not to be optimistic about its duration, and he opens hurriedly:

> Barons, écoutez un excellent couplet.

In the sixth section the poor man is at the end both of his wits and of his patience:

> Seigneurs, pour l'amour de Dieu, faites silence, écoutez moi,
> Pour qu'en partant de ce monde vous entriez dans un meilleur.

Now to meet this difficulty the reciter must either adopt the somewhat apologetic method of the *Chanson d'Antioche*, and wait upon his audience; or he must descend upon them with an impact so sudden that it imposes silence. But, having secured attention, how is he to hold it? In the first place he must have a metre which is easily recitable, which will ring in the ears of the audience, and keep them under the spell. The metre must, therefore, have a pronounced rhythm, and must never be in danger of sounding like prose. It must also possess certain other qualities. It must be powerful in movement, sweeping the audience irresistibly from point to point; and it must be capable of being used for all manner of different purposes; to describe the clash of armies and the turmoil of great fights; a woman weaving, or a group of girls playing ball; the clang of Apollo's silver bow, or the harp song in the place of snakes; the pleadings of a father for his dead son, or the farewell of the two great lovers upon Hindfell.

Further, the reciter must know intimately the technical details of his subject, since he is talking to an audience to whom such details are the commonplaces of daily life, and who will have, therefore, an unsparing eye for inaccuracies. I imagine that the effect of the recital of the Homeric battles upon the Homeric audience, or of Roland's last fight upon the Barons of France—when they listened—or of *Chevy Chase* upon its own audience, was much the same in kind, to compare great things with small, as the effect produced upon the modern athlete by that description of a football or cricket match with which the conventional school story used to be adorned; or upon a boxer by the description of a prize fight; or, on a higher literary plane, upon a hunting man by *Reynard the Fox*. The reader is in the field or the ring himself, criticizing each move with the expert's knowledge. If he is being properly stirred he is keeping up a running fire of detailed praise or blame, and when he reaches the end he is breathless. But just as in these cases it will not do to talk of a brilliant glide to cover, or a hard upper cut to the solar plexus, or to affix to either fox or hound such a merely generic appendage as a 'tail,'[1] so in the battle of the primitive epic what the audience wants is not general atmosphere—that is too familiar to them to be worth creating—but particularity of detail, and correct detail, in which they take a keen and critical

[1] Miss D. L. Sayers, e.g., the most painstaking of writers in such recondite things as the details of campanology, must have irritated many of her readers by an account of a cricket match in which her hero perpetrates three glaring impossibilities.

professional interest. If a spear is said to strike a man where
death comes most quickly to mortal men, it must strike him
where the fighters in the audience have seen death so come. If
Hector takes a spear in hand it will be feeble merely to call it
long; call it ἑνδεκάπηχυ (eleven cubits) and it will convey
something to the audience, like the weight of a tennis racket, or
the difference between a number 2 and a number 5 iron. If
there is a chariot race, it will be no waste of time to include the
long and elaborately professional instructions of Nestor to his
son as to the precise tactics to be adopted at the turning point.[1]
If the reciter were addressing a different audience, one without
first-hand experience, they would probably find the particularity
of detail tedious, inaccuracies would not be noticed, and a
general atmosphere of blood and excitement would suffice.

If the attention of the audience is not to be lost, there must
not be a moment's tedium, for once lost it will hardly be
regained. Hence the need for rise and fall in the narrative, for
dramatic moments, crises, speeches interspersed, adornments,
and digressions. If the audience have had enough of one
character, another must be introduced; or the first character
can tell a story about his grandfather, and after the interested
exploration of this backwater we return with renewed impatience
to the main stream, And even in the straightforward course of
narrative, we can have the minor diversion of similes. But it is
worth remarking that in primitive epic the similes are used
solely to make the narrative more vivid; they are never mere
adornment.

Finally, the reciter must be utterly convinced of the truth of
what he is narrating, or his task is hopeless. I do not mean the
historic truth, since presumably no rhapsode would have drunk
hemlock for his faith in the wanderings of Odysseus, but the
essential truth of his story. The figures of his tale must be as
real to him as his best friend, and the scenes as real as his own
hearthstone, or he will never make them real to his audience.
He must be in the hut of Achilles when Priam enters; and in the
Cyclops' cave apprehensively expecting himself to be the next
for supper; he must watch Sigurd's face change as Brynhild
comes up the hall, and stand by Hogni's side in the last great
battle in the halls of Atli; he must sink into the untroubled

[1] *Iliad*, xxiii. 306–48.

sleep of despair as he waits for the coming of Grendel, and watch in suspense for the emergence of Beowulf from the mere.

But as a partial offset to these disadvantages, the reciter has one signal advantage. He is speaking to an audience; and therefore upon that audience he can exert the full power of the living voice. He can ensure his own—and, if he is competent, the right—interpretation of the poem. The man who writes a poem to be read has to rely upon the interpretation of the reader, which may be to any degree faulty. The reader may be lazy or stupid; he may in his mind emphasize the wrong words, or completely miss the subtleties on which the poet lavished such pains. But the reciter, if he can rely upon his own voice, can ensure that nothing is lost. Anyone who has ever heard a poem, with which he thought himself familiar, read aloud by a really great reader, knows what unimagined beauties are thereby revealed.

To illustrate the qualities of primitive Epic I propose to take four examples; the English and Scottish Border Ballads, the Icelandic Sagas, *Sigurd the Volsung*, and Homer. Someone may object that it is not fair to describe these without reservations as examples of primitive epic, since the first, though primitive, are not epic in form; the second are indeed primitive and epic, but not in verse; the third is epic and in verse, but not chronologically primitive; and the fourth, though epic, and in verse, and early in date, has certain technical leanings towards literary epic. But at least they are all examples of the true spirit of primitive epic, and the fourth has been commonly regarded as the supreme achievement in this form.

Let us begin, then, in a humble way with the Border Ballads, and take as an example of them *Chevy Chase*. I mean the real *Chevy Chase*, not the shoddy fustian counterfeit of later years. Sir Philip Sidney's tribute is almost too well known to quote, but it is a fine thing in itself, and its author had no need to be apologetic about his enthusiasm.[1] 'I never heard the old song of Percy and Douglas, that I found not my heart moved more than with a trumpet.' The old song has the characteristic epic note, the proposal of a single combat between the champions; it has the catalogue of the warriors; it has the rhapsode's trick of

[1] Though it is regrettably probable that he had the later and inferior version before him.

stopping in the middle for a rest, or perhaps while the hat went round. And it rises, at one point at least, to a considerable poetic height.

> The Persè lened on his brand
>   And sawe the Duglas de;
> He tooke the dede man be the hande,
>   And sayd, 'Wo ys me for the!
> To have savyd thy lyf I wold have perted with
>   My landes for yeres thre,
> For a better man of hert, nor of hande,
>   Was not in all the north countré.

The poem as a whole has a well-marked metre, it has rapidity of movement, it has technical detail, and it has human interest. It is a story of warfare told to warriors with trenchant simplicity; it includes the death of a great fighter, and the tribute to him of his great foe. It has the authentic note of primitive epic, and it is typical of the Lays from which the *Iliad* may have sprung. But it is jerky in metre and clumsy in phrasing, so that no audience could listen to it for long; in brief, it is not the work of a great artist, it is not great poetry, and so not great epic. The true comment on it is the conclusion of Sir Philip Sidney's remark, which is too often omitted. 'I never heard the old song of Percy and Douglas, that I found not my heart moved more than with a trumpet; and yet is it sung but by some blind crowder, with no rougher voice than rude style: which being so evil apparelled in the dust and cobwebs of that uncivil age, what would it work trimmed in the gorgeous eloquence of Pindar?' Substitute Homer for Pindar, and suggest to any classical scholar that he answer Sir Philip Sidney's question by turning the passage quoted above into Homeric hexameters. I have seen it done, and I assure you the rendering might have come straight from the greatest book of the *Iliad*.

I wish we could spend longer over these old Ballads. They have a curious strong beauty of their own, as well as great historical interest. I wish still more that we could digress into a full consideration of the Icelandic Sagas, by far the greatest of the epics of the North. They keep all the strength and simplicity of the old songs like the *Lay of Brynhild*, but they are the work of great artists. I will give just one instance, and you will feel, I think, the same note as that of the Ballads, but with it a greater power and weight.

Now when they were come near to the house they knew not whether Gunnar were at home, and bade that some one would go straight up to the house and see if he could find out. But the rest sat them down on the ground.

Thorgrim the Easterling went and began to climb up on the hall; Gunnar sees that a red kirtle passed before the windowslit, and thrusts out the bill, and smote him on the middle. Thorgrim's feet slipped from under him, and he dropped his shield, and down he toppled from the roof.

Then he goes to Gizur and his band as they sat on the ground.

Gizur looked at him and said, 'Well, is Gunnar at home?'

'Find that out for yourselves,' said Thorgrim; 'but this I am sure of, that his bill is at home,' and with that he fell down dead.

Then they made for the buildings. Gunnar shot out arrows at them, and made a stout defence, and they could get nothing done. Then some of them got into the out-houses and tried to attack him thence, but Gunnar found them out with his arrows there also, and still they could get nothing done.

So it went on for a while, then they took a rest, and made a second onslaught. Gunnar still shot out at them, and they could do nothing, and fell off the second time. Then Gizur the White said, 'Let us press on harder; nothing comes of our onslaught.'

Then they made a third bout of it, and were long at it, and then they fell off again.

Gunnar said, 'There lies an arrow outside on the wall, and it is one of their shafts; I will shoot at them with it, and it will be a shame to them if they get a hurt from their own weapons.'

His mother said, 'Do not so my son; nor rouse them again when they have already fallen off from the attack.'

But Gunnar caught up the arrow and shot it after them, and struck Eylif Aunund's son, and he got a great wound; he was standing all by himself, and they knew not that he was wounded.

'Out came an arm yonder,' says Gizur, 'and there was a
gold ring on it, and took an arrow from the roof, and they
would not look outside for shafts if there were enough
indoors; and now ye shall make a fresh onslaught.'

'Let us burn him house and all,' said Mord.[1]

That is magnificently strong, untinselled narration—but it
has no metre. Now let us see what happens when to plain
simplicity of thought and strong simplicity of feeling is added
the emotional effect of powerful metre.

I want to bring before you one of the most interesting, and I
think one of the most undeservedly neglected, works in all
English literature. It puts into English verse one of the most
moving of the primitive epics of the North. The man who wrote
it was by instinct himself primitive, born many hundred years
out of his due time; he was steeped in the old sagas, and he was
a great craftsman. And I believe the result to be that, as we
have in our language the greatest literary epic, so we have also
one of the greatest primitive verse epics, in the literature of
Europe, *Sigurd the Volsung*. I do not think that either the *Song of
Roland* or *Beowulf* can equal it. Indeed, for the sheer sweep and
grandeur of its story, *Sigurd* is at least equal to the *Iliad* and
superior to the *Odyssey*, though it falls short both of them and
the prose sagas in continuous vividness of presentation, as it
falls short, though not far short, of the *Iliad* in magnificence of
style.

This may seem an extravagant estimate. Of readers who
know the poem, some, though I hope only a few, will think it
worse than extravagant. They do not find in the poem the bare
unadorned force which they find and value in the prose sagas;
they feel perhaps that just because Morris was writing in the
nineteenth century there must be something bogus about the
poem; and I fancy that the very power of the metre, with its
rapid and compulsive sweep, decoys them into thinking that
the narrative is more diffuse than in fact it is. Others, perhaps

---

[1] *The Story of Burnt Njal* (trans. Sir George Dasent).

I would refer those who wish to follow this side of the subject
further to W. P. Ker's *Epic and Romance*, and also to Chadwick's
The Heroic Age. In particular no one can afford to omit, in connection
with any study of epic, the masterly chapter in *Epic and Romance* on
'the Art of Narrative.'

wiser, and certainly more fortunate, who have once surrendered to the poem's power, and for whom no amount of re-reading can weaken or stale it, will be less ready to dismiss my estimate as absurd. But all readers to whom *Sigurd* is no more than a name will very rightly be demanding some reasons in support of the estimate.

First then, *Sigurd* has an epic metre, strong, rapid, easily variable, and, though not directly intended for that purpose, very apt for recitation. If you sit down to read *Sigurd*, you will find that you are very soon reading it aloud; not mentally aloud, as anyone with an ear as a matter of course reads poetry, but actually aloud. You may be thinking that I stress unduly the importance of metre. I doubt whether its importance can be unduly stressed, and I am sure that it is usually unduly neglected, relegated to the sphere of the merely technical, of the things which are all very well in their way for pedantic persons who like to measure poetry with a foot-rule and enjoy the jargon of Trochees and Anapaests and Pyrrhics, but which are quite irrelevant to the real appreciation of poetry. If you do not care to take my word for it that this is not so, may I suggest that Saintsbury, whatever one may think of his merits or demerits as a critic—and most of us have strong views—was hardly a pedantic person; and that two of his most substantial contributions to English criticism were both concerned with rhythm, namely *A History of English Prosody* and *A History of English Prose Rhythm*? The truth of the matter is this; we have to admit, whether we like it or not, that at least a part, and perhaps a great part, of the emotional effect of poetry is a musical effect. Part of this musical effect depends, no doubt, on the sound values of the words themselves, the shifting vowel sounds, the particular successions of consonants; these correspond, if you like, to the notes in music; but part of the effect, both in music and poetry, depends upon something much more primitive in its appeal, upon a recurrent beat, which we call the time in music, and the rhythm or metre in poetry. And a particular metre or time has a perfectly definite and particular effect upon the emotional temper of the reader or hearer. So definite is the effect that the choice of an unsuitable metre for a poem of a particular type almost certainly dooms the poem to failure, because the effect of the metre and the effect of the sense of the words are antagonistic where they should be harmonious. Byron, for example, had a favourite jerky light-cavalry anapaestic metre, which served admirably for describing the descent of the Assyrian; and he tried to write love lyrics in the same metre, with the deplorable results which we know.[1] Whereas nothing could be more perfect than the ottava rima of *Don Juan* for the gamin's trick which Byron took such a delight in playing so often in the final couplet. And not only does the metre affect the hearer, but it is probable that it affects the poet, so that his mental processes work in one way in one metre, and in a different way in another. It would probably be impossible to write a primitive epic in English blank verse because it would be impossible to make the movement sufficiently rapid. (That, by the way, is one reason why so many translations of Homer are unsatisfactory.) Let me try to illustrate by an example the complete change of tone that is caused by a change of metre. We all know the peculiar effect of *Paradise Lost*, its weight, its grandeur, its air of a brocade stiff with gold. Let us try an experiment. I wish we could get Kingsley to do it for us, for he was the only real master of the English hexameter of the ordinary accentual type, as Robert Bridges was the only master of the quantitative; but we must do the best we can. Here are the opening lines of *Paradise Lost* as Milton wrote them:

> Of Man's first disobedience, and the fruit
> Of that forbidden tree, whose mortal taste
> Brought death into the world, and all our woe,

> .   .   .   .   .

> Sing Heavenly Muse.

Here is the same sense transposed into another metre:

> Sing, O Muse, of the first disobedience of Man, and the
>   mortal
> Taste of the fruit forbidden, which brought death into
>   the world, and
> All our woe.

[1] Cf. 'The Assyrian came down like a wolf on the fold' with 'Oh Fame, if I e'er took delight in thy praises.'

Here is the opening of one of Milton's famous similes:

> Thick as autumnal leaves that strow the brooks
> In Vallombrosa

Try it thus:

> Thick as autumnal leaves that in Vallombrosa
>   descending
> Strow the brooks,

That, if I may say so, is a not bad English hexameter, but it is not Milton, nor anything like Milton. Or again, for the opposite contrast, compare Homer's account of Achilles shouting over the trench with Tennyson's grand translation, stately, sonorous, as splendid as blank verse can be. But the one is the athlete stripped and at full speed, straining for the goal, the other the same athlete moving slowly to receive his crown.[1]

To return from this digression to the metre of *Sigurd*. As a primitive epic metre must be, it is rapid in movement, marked in rhythm, and capable of great variety. Morris used it with astonishing skill. It is a metre which may at any moment degenerate into the worst and most wearisome doggerel. And not once, through four long books, does it so degenerate. It might become merely monotonous, and one is perpetually being delighted by the changes which are rung upon it. Many metres have the lulling sway of a small boat on a gentle swell: here for the most part is the thrust and 'scend of a great ship shouldering through a sea. But the metre can change also to the most delicate tenderness. Let me give you a taste of it in a passage which is good, but not above the general level:

> Then into the Volsung dwelling a mighty man there strode,
> One-eyed and seeming ancient, yet bright his visage glowed:
> Cloud-blue was the hood upon him, and his kirtle gleaming-
>   grey
> As the latter morning sundog when the storm is on the way:
> A bill he bore on his shoulder, whose mighty ashen beam
> Burnt bright with the flame of the sea and the blended
>   silver's gleam.

[1] *Iliad*, xviii. 202–29.
Achilles over the Trench: 'So saying, light-foot Iris passed away . . .'

And such was the guise of his raiment as the Volsung
    elders had told
Was borne by their fathers' fathers, and the first that warred
    in the wold.[1]

Or for a different note:

On went the Volsung banners, and on went Sigmund before,
And his sword was the flail of the tiller on the wheat of the
    wheat-thrashing floor,
And his shield was rent from his arm, and his helm was
    sheared from his head:
But who may draw nigh him to smite for the heap and the
    rampart of dead?[2]

Or, for the softer melody, take the farewell of Sigurd and
Brynhild on Hindfell:

From his hand then draweth Sigurd Andvari's ancient gold;
There is nought but the sky above them as the ring together
    they hold,
The shapen ancient token, that hath no change nor end,
No change, and no beginning, no flaw for God to mend:
Then Sigurd cries: 'O Brynhild, now hearken while I swear
That the sun shall die in the heavens and the day no more
    be fair,
If I seek not love in Lymdale and the house that fostered
    thee,
And the land where thou awakedst 'twixt the woodland and
    the sea!'
And she cried: 'O Sigurd, Sigurd, now hearken while I swear
That the day shall die for ever and the sun to blackness wear,
Ere I forget thee, Sigurd, as I lie 'twixt wood and sea
In the little land of Lymdale and the house that fostered
    me!'[3]

Or, for sheer technical brilliance, take the four lines in which
the melody of Gunnar's harp rises to his death song. May I ask
you to notice, in particular, how at the word 'orderly' the
purposely uneasy movement of the first two lines and a half
shifts to measured music?—

[1] Book I, 1st section.   [2] *Ibid*, last section but two.
[3] Book II, close to the end.

Then he rose at once to his feet, and smote the harp with his
    hand,
And it rang as if with a cry in the dream of a lonely land;
Then he fondled its wail as it faded, and orderly over the
    strings
Went the marvellous sound of its sweetness, like the march
    of Odin's kings.[1]

Those illustrations are perhaps enough to show that if the
subject is great and greatly handled, here is a metre that will
not fall below it.

What then of the subject of the poem and its structure?
The structure has been harshly criticized, mainly by critics who
cavil at the poem for not being something which it was never
intended to be. It is true that Sigurd is not born till the beginning
of Book II, and dies at the end of Book III. But it is not true that
Books I and IV are therefore irrelevant. The critics would be
wiser if they would look at the full title of the poem, *Sigurd the
Volsung, and the Fall of the Niblungs*. The subject of the epic is not
the story of two individuals, however great; it is the story of the
destruction of two great royal houses. The first book sets the
stage, and a vast stage, for the entrance of the last and greatest
of the Volsungs. Then through two books we follow the love and
deaths of Sigurd and Brynhild to the tremendous climax of the
third book. But the narrator will not stop there; he goes on
remorselessly till the sin of Sigurd's killing is washed out by the
blood that flowed in the hall of Atli; and Gudrun, who brought
the sorrow, has seen Sigurd avenged, and followed him and her
brothers; and the Niblung race is ended, and the whole tale
told, that began when Sigmund sailed with his Volsungs to their
doom. The epic might be more acceptable to modern taste if it
opened with Sigurd's birth and closed as the flames rise from
his pyre. And if it were the writer's aim to concentrate attention
exclusively upon the two central figures and their tragic history,
no doubt by this contraction of the stage, this focusing of the
limelight, he would most readily achieve his aim. But the epic
so constructed would be a miserably smaller thing. It is just
because the tale of Sigurd and Brynhild, grand and deeply
moving as it is, is felt to be, for all its intensity and power, no

[1] Book IV, last section but one.

more than an episode in a vaster and overwhelming history that the poem has its peculiar grandeur. I doubt whether there is any other poem in English which so completely sweeps the reader off his feet by the conjoined strength and splendour of its music and its imagination. You are out and away from the rich galleries of the Palace of Art, among great mountains, in the storm and sun of an earlier heroic world; and against that background, wherein move dimly the stern figures of the old Norse mythology, is worked out a story of love, and hatred, and death, as great as any in the literature of the world. The poem has an unmistakably Northern quality; there is magic about, and mystery, Grimhild's potion and the wolf men; we are troubled by a sense of fate, brooding, irresistible, before which even the heroic Sigurd is powerless. The mists are low on the hills, and we have often to strain our eyes to catch the outlines of things through the storm wrack; but now and again the clouds break, and under the rainbow arch in the sudden sun-light we catch glimpses of surpassing loveliness.

May we end our cursory examination of this poem with two passages from the third book? For those who are not familiar with it, I must give the barest outline of this part of the story. Sigurd, riding homewards from the conquest of the treasure of the Dwarf Andvari, comes to Hindfell and its ring of fire. He rides the flames and finds Brynhild sleeping. He wakens her, and hears her story, how she had been Odin's victory-wafter, till for some disobedience he imprisoned her in sleep behind the flame-wall, till a man should be found to ride it. They pledge their love and bid farewell in a passage from which I quoted earlier. Sigurd comes to the Niblungs. Their king's daughter Gudrun falls in love with him; her mother Grimhild prepares a potion which Sigurd unwittingly drinks; his heart is changed, Brynhild is forgotten, and he marries Gudrun. As the cup is drunk, Brynhild in Lymdale is again prisoned behind the flame-wall. News of this imprisoned maiden comes to the Niblungs, and Gudrun's brother Gunnar, now Sigurd's blood-brother, rides to woo her. But when neither will his horse face the flames, nor Sigurd's with him in the saddle, Sigurd changes semblances with him, and rides the fire in the outward guise of the Niblung, to win for him his own old love. Brynhild, thus won, comes to the Niblung town to wed Gunnar. On the marriage day she is led

up the great hall towards the high seat where Sigurd sits: and
as he looks, suddenly the force of the potion is ended, and the
past is real again, and he knows the truth:

Then the Wise-wife hushed before her, and a little fell aside,
And nought from the eyes of Brynhild the high-seat now did
      hide;
And the face so long desired, unchanged from time agone,
In the house of the Cloudy People from the Niblung high-
      seat shone:
She stood with her hand in Gunnar's, and all about and
      around
Were the unfamiliar faces, and the folk that day had found;
But her heart ran back through the years, and yet her lips
      did move
With the words she spake on Hindfell, when they plighted
      troth of love.

Lo, Sigurd fair on the high-seat by the white-armed Gudrun's
      side,
In the midst of the Cloudy People, in the dwelling of their
      pride!
His face is exceeding glorious and awful to behold;
For of all his sorrow he knoweth and his hope smit dead and
      cold:
The will of the Norns is accomplished, and, lo, they wend
      on their ways,
And leave the mighty Sigurd to deal with the latter days:
The Gods look down from Heaven, and the lonely King
      they see,
And sorrow over his sorrow, and rejoice in his majesty.
For the will of the Norns is accomplished, and outworn is
      Grimhild's spell,
And nought now shall blind or help him, and the tale shall
      be to tell:
He hath seen the face of Brynhild, and he knows why she
      hath come,
And that his is the hand that hath drawn her to the Cloudy
      People's home:
He knows of the net of the days, and the deeds that the Gods
      have bid,

And no whit of the sorrow that shall be from his wakened
    soul is hid:
And his glory his heart restraineth, and restraineth the hand
    of the strong
From the hope of the fools of desire and the wrong that
    amendeth wrong;
And he seeth the ways of the burden till the last of the
    uttermost end.
But for all the measureless anguish, and the woe that nought
    may amend,
His heart speeds back to Hindfell, and the dawn of the
    wakening day;
And the hours betwixt are as nothing, and their deeds are
    fallen away
As he looks on the face of Brynhild; and nought is the Niblung
    folk,
But they two are again together, and he speaketh the words
    he spoke,
When he swore the love that endureth, and the truth that
    knoweth not change;
And Brynhild's face drew near him with eyes grown stern
    and strange.
—Lo, such is the high Gods' sorrow, and men know nought
    thereof,
Who cry out o'er their undoing, and wail o'er broken love.
Now she stands on the floor of the high-seat, and for e'en so
    little a space
As men may note delaying, she looketh on Sigurd's face,
Ere she saith: 'I have greeted many in the Niblungs' house
    today,
And for thee is the last of my greetings ere the feast shall
    wear away:
Hail, Sigurd, son of the Volsungs! hail lord of Odin's
    storm!
Hail rider of the wasteland and slayer of the Worm!
If aught thy soul shall desire while yet thou livest on earth,
I pray that thou mayst win it, nor forget its might and worth.'

All grief, sharp scorn, sore longing, stark death in her voice
    he knew,

> But gone forth is the doom of the Norns, and what shall he
>   answer thereto,
> While the death that amendeth lingers? and they twain shall
>   dwell for awhile
> In the Niblung house together by the hearth that forged the
>   guile;
> Yet amid the good and the guileless, and the love that
>   thought no wrong,
> Shall they fashion the deeds to remember, and the fame that
>   endureth for long.

You will travel long and far in the realms of gold before you match that scene for power and restraint. And it is full of the Northern melancholy, the yearning at man's pitiful helplessness before the inscrutable mysteries of fate. But let us go on to the climax. When the truth of the wooing is revealed to Brynhild by Gudrun in a fit of passion, the Niblung brothers, for some reason not adequately explained, determine that Sigurd must die. He is killed by the youngest of the brothers and Brynhild prepares to follow him:

> But Brynhild cried to her maidens: 'Now open ark and
>   chest,
> And draw forth queenly raiment of the loveliest and the best,
> Red rings that the Dwarf-lords fashioned, fair cloths that
>   queens have sewed
> To array the bride for the mighty, and the traveller for the
>   road.
>
>   .   .   .   .   .
>
> Now give me the sword, O maidens, wherewith I sheared
>   the wind
> When the Kings of Earth were gathered to know the
>   Chooser's mind.'

She sends to summon Gunnar and drives the sword home. When he comes she makes her prayer:

> 'I pray thee a prayer, the last word in the world I speak,
> That ye bear me forth to Sigurd, and the hand my hand
>   would seek;
> The bale for the dead is builded, it is wrought full wide on
>   the plain,

It is raised for Earth's best Helper, and thereon is room for
    twain:
Ye have hung the shields about it, and the Southland
    hangings spread,
There lay me adown by Sigurd and my head beside his
    head:
But ere ye leave us sleeping, draw his Wrath from out the
    sheath,
And lay that Light of the Branstock, and the blade that
    frighted death
Betwixt my side and Sigurd's, as it lay that while agone,
When once in one bed together we twain were laid alone:
How then when the flames flare upward may I be left
    behind?
How then may the road he wendeth be hard for my feet to
    find?
How then in the gates of Valhall may the door of the gleam-
    ing ring
Clash to on the heel of Sigurd, as I follow on my king?'

That is the culminating peak which we cross in our passage
along the mountain range of Sigurd; but we never drop very
far below that level. That is immeasurably greater poetry than
the rough vigour of the ballads or the crude strength of *Beowulf*.
It may indeed challenge comparison with any primitive epic of
Europe except one. And that one is serenely *hors concours*.

I do not know that we can do better than preface our
examination of Homer by reading one of the loveliest of
modern sonnets, prefixed to a translation of the lesser of the two
great Homeric epics:

    As one that for a weary space has lain
        Lulled by the song of Circe and her wine,
        In gardens near the pale of Proserpine,
    Where that Aeaean isle forgets the main,
    And only the low lutes of love complain,
        And only shadows of wan lovers pine;
        As such an one were glad to know the brine
    Salt on his lips, and the large air again—
    So gladly, from the songs of modern speech
        Men turn, and see the stars, and feel the free

> Shrill wind beyond the close of heavy flowers;
> And through the music of the languid hours,
> They hear like ocean on a western beach
> The surge and thunder of the Odyssey.[1]

Again, you see, the metre in the forefront of the poet's appeal. And no wonder, the Homeric hexameter being beyond question, if not the most magnificent, at least the strongest, swiftest, and most compelling metre in the European languages.[2] For all its swiftness it is dignified, and for all its strength it is infinitely variable, but never merely facile. In the ordinary passages we are riding smoothly on the swell, but when something more is needed we are suddenly caught and carried out to sea on an irresistible current of sound. To change the picture, Homer's flight is always lofty, but when the moment comes to

[1] Andrew Lang.

[2] But it is only honest to point out that Aristotle makes comments on the hexameter metre which seem to us very unexpected. He says that of all metres it is ὀγκωδέστατον. There is no doubt what that means—the 'heaviest,' the 'weightiest.' And we may without much difficulty accept that, though it is perhaps hardly the word we should have chosen. But he also describes it as στασιμώτατον. And that we find really puzzling, since, though the meaning of the word is not so precise as that of the other, it is clearly something to do with 'standing,' so that 'stationary' would be near it—i.e. almost the precise opposite of 'rapid.' And this suggests some interesting speculations as to how the Greeks really *heard* their metres, and as to the differences between quantitative and accentual scansions. We hear our metres almost entirely in terms of recurrent stresses and of the number of unstressed syllables which intervene between them. To our ears therefore a dactylic line (e.g. 'Leaping the gulfs of the surge, as he laughed in the joy of his leaping'*) is rapid in movement because each stress is followed by two unstressed syllables, and this produces for us a tripping, dancing effect, like the rhythm of a waltz. And we are apt to read a Greek hexameter in the same way (e.g. any of the four lines of Alcman on p. 11), putting a stress on the 'long' syllables, putting as little weight as possible on the 'short' syllables, and so maintaining the same rapid effect. Of course we know in theory that two short syllables are 'equivalent to' one long one, but we make not the least attempt to *hear* them so in practice. But it is at least arguable that the Greeks did so hear them, and, if they did, the hexameter measure was to them a series of feet which either were, or were felt as, spondees, and it was therefore to their ears what Aristotle calls it.

* Kingsley, *Andromeda*.

soar, there is no poet who rises with such strong and utterly effortless exultation, with so little beating of the wings. Here is one short passage of Homer by no means at his highest, though perhaps somewhat above his ordinary narrative level. A reader who has no Greek must, I am afraid, be content to find someone to read it aloud, for to anyone with an ear there is pleasure in the sound alone. It is the famous three lines describing the nod of Zeus when the ambrosial locks roll down round the immortal head and great Olympus trembles:

ἦ καὶ κυανέῃσιν ἐπ᾽ ὀφρύσι νεῦσε Κρονίων·
ἀμβρόσιαι δ᾽ ἄρα χαῖται ἐπερρώσαντο ἄνακτος
κρατὸς ἀπ᾽ ἀθανάτοιο· μέγαν δ᾽ ἐλέλιξεν Ὄλυμπον[1]

So much for the metre: for the rest, since any vague eulogy of such works as the *Iliad* and the *Odyssey* is the worst of critical futilities, I shall try to suggest certain definite qualities which are characteristic of Homer, and in varying degrees characteristic also of *Sigurd* and other primitive epics.

It is, by the way, inevitable that one should use the word 'Homer,' and it is a very convenient term for that body of work which is traditionally Homer's, so long as it is understood that even the use of the singular preposition 'he' with reference to 'Homer' does not imply any particular view as to single or multiple authorship, but is simply a convenience to avoid sentences of a cumbrously legal type, like, 'He (or, if there was more than one author, they, or in this case at least some of them) was (or were) . . . ,' and so on. For our purpose it is of almost negligible importance whether 'Homer' was written by one man or by twenty, or whether one poet of supreme genius combined, with additions of his own, existing scattered fragments. But a good deal of nonsense is talked with a superior air by the less scholarly supporters of the single authorship, and for any English reader who wants to read and appreciate the *Iliad as a whole*, whether in the original or in translation, it is a real help to just appreciation if he is aware at least what the problem is.[2] For the moment, however, let us confine our attention to the work itself, however few or many authors it had, and examine some of its characteristics.

[1] *Iliad*, i. 528–30.
[2] See Gilbert Murray, *The Rise of the Greek Epic*.

In the first place, then, there is in these two great epics an arresting simplicity of thought and outlook. This does not mean that the diction is plain. Far from it; but it is an elementary confusion which correlates simplicity of thought and simplicity of diction. As you find one of the subtlest of philosophers expressing himself with a Quakerish perfection of plainness, so here you find the most magnificently polysyllabic and ornate vocabulary used to clothe the plainest thinking. Characters and actions are all straightforward and life is reduced to its simplest terms. Homer never philosophizes, never speculates, never rebels. He has that temper towards life which character-ized many of the great Greeks, a 'noble acquiescence.' It is the temper of Sophocles. No doubt there are many questions which might be asked. Why did Thetis bear Achilles ὠκυμορώτατον ἄλλων (shortest-lived of heroes)? Why is the race of man as swiftly fading as the race of leaves?[1] But time spent over such questions is time wasted. Time should be spent in living, not in speculating about life. Achilles *is* ὠκυμορώτατος, and the race of men *is* like the race of leaves, and that is all about it. Life is in front of the Homeric heroes to be lived and fought through. In the end comes death and a shadowy existence. You remember the answer of the spirit of Achilles to Odysseus?

μὴ δή μοι θάνατόν γε παραύδα, φαίδιμ' 'Οδυσσεῦ.
βουλοίμην κ' ἐπάρουρος ἐὼν θητευέμεν ἄλλῳ
ἀνδρὶ παρ' ἀκλήρῳ, ᾧ μὴ βίοτος πολὺς εἴη,
ἢ πᾶσιν νεκύεσσι καταφθιμένοισιν ἀνάσσειν.[2]

Life after death is no life, and 'the fates of death stand about us every way and no mortal may escape them.' Tomorrow we die; but the corollary is not so much 'let us eat and drink' as ἴομεν 'let us go forward, whether we give glory to other men or others to us.'[3] It is an attitude which resolves many complications. You will notice that there is here none of the Northern brooding, none of the sense of mystery. In the Northern epics we get a hint of the blank misgivings of a creature moving about in worlds

---

[1] οἵη περ φύλλων γενεή, τοίη δὲ καὶ ἀνδρῶν. *Iliad*, vi. 146.

[2] *Odyssey*, xi. 488–91. 'Do not try to make death less grievous, noble Odysseus. I would choose to be the bond-slave of another man, and he portionless and with a scant livelihood, so I were still on earth, rather than be king over all the dead that are perished.'

[3] *Iliad*, xii. 326–8.

not realized; and in a famous Virgilian line you find a kindred
sense of unsatisfied desire. But the temper of which Homer is
typical is one which is determined that its world shall be fully
realized, even if that realization can be secured only by a
rigorous contraction of the boundaries.

You will notice in Homer the characteristic Greek restraint
which likes to produce its strongest effects by understatement
or by indirect and apparently inadequate statement. The queen
of the Laestrygones, says Homer, was as big as the peak of a
mountain. There is no expatiation on her enormity; κατὰ δ'
ἔστυγον αὐτήν,[1] 'and they loathed her.' (Incidentally, there
you have a light on the Greeks' love of the normal, their hatred
of monstrosity.) Or take a line like τὸ πρὶν ἐπ' εἰρήνης, πρὶν
ἐλθεῖν υἷας Ἀχαιῶν,[2] the war-weariness of a great city concentrated in eight words, and a more memorable line than several of
Matthew Arnold's touchstones. Or take the most notable instance of all, the cause of the war. Many inferior writers,
wanting to bring a beautiful woman before you, are apt to
compile a kind of auctioneer's catalogue of her charms;
and the result is about as attractive. Watch the real artist
at work. Different though they are in method, the one
exuberant, the other restrained, the instinct of Marlowe[3]
and Homer is the same, to describe beauty indirectly
by its effects. The old men at Troy sit on the wall, chattering
like grasshoppers, and the woman passes whose fatal beauty
has brought ten years of misery to them and their kindred, and
doomed their great city to destruction in the end. The poet takes
the chance, not to describe Helen, but to pay her 'the most
tremendous tribute beauty ever won':

οὐ νέμεσις Τρῶας καὶ ἐϋκνήμιδας Ἀχαιοὺς
τοιῆδ' ἀμφὶ γυναικὶ πολὺν χρόνον ἄλγεα πάσχειν·
αἰνῶς ἀθανάτῃσι θεῇς εἰς ὦπα ἔοικεν.[4]

Let us not miss the full power of those lines. You may find them
travestied, and by a professor of English who ought to have

[1] *Odyssey*, x. 113.
[2] *Iliad*, xxii. 156. 'In the old days of peace before ever the Achaeans
came.'
[3] 'Was this the face that launch'd a thousand ships,
   And burn'd the topless towers of Ilium?'
[4] *Iliad*, iii. 156–8.

known better, as 'No wonder that the young men fight for her.' Many an ordinary reigning toast might have had that remark made about her. What the old men in Homer say is 'One cannot blame them that for such a woman as this two great nations endure long years of the travail of war for'—the poet avoids the danger—'she has the awful beauty of the immortals.'

You will find in Homer pathos, strong and dignified, whether it is the lament Andromache over Hector,[1] or the lines which explain why Helen could not see her brothers among the Greek chieftains:

$$\overset{‿}{\omega}_{S} \ \phi\acute{a}\tau o, \ \tau o\grave{v}_{S} \ \delta' \ \mathring{\eta}\delta\eta \ \kappa\acute{a}\tau\epsilon\chi\epsilon\nu \ \phi\upsilon\sigma\acute{\iota}\zeta oo_{S} \ a\mathring{\iota}a$$
$$\mathring{\epsilon}\nu \ \Lambda a\kappa\epsilon\delta a\acute{\iota}\mu o\nu\iota \ a\mathring{v}\theta\iota, \ \phi\acute{\iota}\lambda\eta \ \mathring{\epsilon}\nu \ \pi a\tau\rho\acute{\iota}\delta\iota \ \gamma a\acute{\iota}\eta.^{2}$$

And you will find humour of several types. There is the somewhat crude type of the episode in which Hephaestus understudies Hebe, and quenchless laughter arises among the blessed gods as they watch him hobbling through the halls;[3] which makes one feel that whatever else the blessed gods may have been they were no gentlemen. And there is the high comedy of much of the doings of the family circle of the immortals, not least Aphrodite's ill-starred attempt to exchange the arts of love for the perils of war.[4] And there is the grim type, which is the commonest in the Northern epic (like the report of Gunnar's bill being at home), represented by the fate of the hanged serving maids in the Odyssey and the line

$$\mathring{\eta}\sigma\pi a\iota\rho o\nu \ \delta\grave{\epsilon} \ \pi\acute{o}\delta\epsilon\sigma\sigma\iota \ \mu\acute{\iota}\nu\upsilon\nu\theta\acute{a} \ \pi\epsilon\rho, \ o\mathring{v} \ \tau\iota \ \mu\acute{a}\lambda a \ \delta\mathring{\eta}\nu^{5}$$

since behind that line—in spite of attempts to find in it an expurgation—is surely concealed the smile which Homer describes as

$$\sigma a\rho\delta\acute{a}\nu\iota o\nu \ \mu\acute{a}\lambda a \ \tau o\mathring{\iota}o\nu$$

(sardonic—very).

---

[1] *Iliad*, xxiv. 723–45.
[2] *Iliad*, iii. 243, 4.
   'So said she;—they long since in Earth's soft arms were reposing,
   There, in their own dear land, their Fatherland, Lacedaemon.'
                                        (Dr. Hawtrey, 1847).
[3] *Iliad*, i. 599, 600.   [4] *Iliad*, v. 311–430.
[5] *Odyssey*, xxii. 473. 'They kicked with their feet for a while—not for long.'

If you demand the vivid presentation of a scene, let Homer present it for you, whether it be the rapid impressionistic sketches of the Shield of Achilles[1] or the full-dress staging of the Ransoming of Hector.[2] Or if you want the delight in the strong and sudden dramatic moment, take the swift transition at the opening of the 22nd book of the Odyssey. It is worth studying this as an example of the finished art of narration. The scene is in the hall of Odysseus. He has come back, disguised as a beggar, to his own home. The suitors have been trying their hands at an old trick of Odysseus', the shooting an arrow through a row of axe-heads. They have failed even to string the great bow, let alone shoot the arrow, and are resting, vexed with their failure. When the old beggar who has been sitting quietly by the great door asks if he may try, they jeer at him, but consent. The scene could hardly be more peaceful. He takes the bow and handles it, turning it in his hands to see whether the worms have eaten it in his long absence. Then, as easily as a man puts a new string in a lyre—one is aware of the value of the quiet pacific simile—he strings the bow, and as he plucks the string with his finger it sings like the voice of a swallow. Then he takes an arrow and shoots it through the axe-heads. The suitors are troubled, and the tension increases as Odysseus makes an ambiguous speech. The thunder clouds are gathering, but, though there is something ominous about the hush, through which is heard the thunder of Zeus, the scene is still quiet, the suitors watching in astonishment, Odysseus sitting where he was when the bow was put into his hands. And then in an instant the storm breaks; and you can hear the gusto in the rhapsode's voice as he launches out on the slaying of the suitors. Listen to the rattling thunder in the fourth word:

αὐτὰρ ὁ γυμνώθη ῥακέων πολύμητις Ὀδυσσεύς.[3]

'But he cast off his rags, Odysseus of many devices, and leapt to the great threshold, holding his bow and quiver full of arrows, and he poured out the swift shafts there at his feet as he spoke to the suitors: "This bloodless trial is ended, and I shall aim at another mark, which no man yet has hit, if I may hit it, and Apollo grant me renown."' And, before a man can move,

---

[1] *Iliad*, xviii.   [2] *Iliad*, xxiv. 478–606.   [3] *Odyssey*, xxii. 1.

Antinous has fallen with an arrow through his throat, and the suitors, even now only half conscious of their doom, are gazing at the great figure on the threshold, motionless and menacing.

When one is once launched on the great sea of Homer it is hard to stop; one wants to sail on out of time and space into the sunset. But we must come back to harbour from the wine-dark sea. May I in conclusion suggest certain points of contrast between Homer and *Sigurd*.

First, in power of characterization Homer leaves *Sigurd* far behind. The great figures in *Sigurd* are no more than crude outlines when you set them beside the gods and men of Homer, sculptured with faultless accuracy and detailed completeness— though marble is far too cold a description of these vivid, warm-blooded, moving figures. From their very incompleteness the figures in *Sigurd* have a grandeur of their own, like a Rodin bronze, but they are removed too far from the ordinary human plane. Further, Homer shares with other creative artists of the very first rank that power which distinguishes them from their inferiors, the power of creating characters who are at once universal types and clear-cut individuals. Hamlet is no doubt a 'type' of all men whose resolution of a critical problem is made agonisingly difficult by a combination of their circumstances and their characters; but he is also Prince of Denmark, and the King's 'mighty opposite.' Nausicaa and Miranda are both 'types' of radiant and lovely maidenhood; but the one is daughter of Prospero, Duke of Milan, and the other of Alcinous, King in Phaeacia. The home-coming of Odysseus is the return of all wanderers; but he is king of craggy Ithaca and Penelope's husband. Whereas Sigurd and Gunnar and Brynhild, and for that matter Skarpheddin and Njal and Roland and Beowulf, are themselves and no more than themselves.

Secondly, everything in Homer is in the light, in the bright, hard sunlight of the south. There is no magic, or at any rate no mystery. Even when supranormal things happen they are accepted as on the normal plane, being as a rule ascribed to the agency of a definite and known god. The Greeks hated the unknown, the dark corners of the mind or the imagination. The cry of Ajax, foiled by the mist which shrouds the battlefield, is indeed the cry of the whole Greek race:

Ζεῦ πάτερ, ἀλλὰ σὺ ῥῦσαι ὑπ' ἠέρος υἷας Ἀχαιῶν,
ποίησον δ' αἴθρην, δὸς δ' ὀφθαλμοῖσιν ἰδέσθαι·
ἐν δὲ φάει καὶ ὄλεσσον.[1]

And lastly I want to bring before you a subject of which I can touch the merest fringe; the Homeric simile. But it is, in one aspect, of great importance, since more perhaps than anything else it differentiates Homer from the northern epic and may also be regarded as the link between Homer and the literary epic. Some indeed would say that it removes Homer from the category of the pure primitive epic. If you examine *Sigurd* or *Burnt Njal* you will find a remarkable paucity of simile. A haphazard selection of ten consecutive pages of *Sigurd* yielded the following: 'Green as the ocean,' which is merely commonplace; 'thy visage gleams like a thing my dream has known,' which is singularly vague; 'unmighty as the tempest-driven straw,' not much more significant; a pillar 'like the waves heart shone,' merely obscure; and two which are vivid but brief:

> dim did his bright shape grow
> As a man from the litten doorway fades into the
> dusk of night,

and

> they felt themselves tangled and caught
> As when the net cometh up before the folk of the firth
> And the main sea lieth far off.

A further haphazard ten pages yielded an even scantier harvest of two similes. And you will notice that all these similes have an air of slipping in by accident; they are not inserted with design; they just happen to occur to the writer as he goes on with his narrative. And in the prose sagas, as one would expect, the difficulty is to find any simile at all. They are the starkest kind of naked tale-telling, though they have a finished art of their own. But now turn to Homer: the speeches have few similes; but take an ordinary passage of narrative like the opening of the third book of the *Iliad*. There in sixty-five lines you will find five full-dress similes, occupying eighteen lines of the sixty-five. Let us take two of these and examine them.

[1] *Iliad*, xvii. 645–7. 'Father Zeus, deliver the sons of the Achaeans from the mist, and make the sky clear above us, and grant us to see with our eyes, and, so that it be in the light, even destroy us.'

The two hosts have advanced across the plain to battle. Paris, fully armed, comes out before the Trojans, and challenges the Greek leaders to meet him in single fight. Then, says Homer,[1] 'when Menelaus saw him striding out before the host, as a lion that rejoices when he lights upon a great carcass, whether of stag or of wild goat, when he is hungry, and he devours it ravenously, in case the swift hounds and the hunters may set upon him, so Menelaus rejoiced when he saw the god-like Paris, for he thought to take vengeance on the sinner, and he leapt from his chariot to the ground. And when Paris saw him suddenly in the front rank, he was afraid, and shrank back among his companions, dreading death; as a man seeing a snake in a woodland thicket starts back trembling and shrinks away and his cheeks grow pale, so Paris drew back into the ranks of Trojans in fear of the son of Atreus.' Now observe: in each case the poet, to illustrate an episode of his narrative, draws a complete picture of an analogous occurrence: the lion is ravenous for food, Menelaus for revenge; each sees unexpectedly what may satisfy the hunger; each, fearing interruption, is in haste to seize the chance; in the second instance the appearance of Menelaus and of the snake is equally sudden; the effect on Paris and on the man is the same: in one passage only is there a detail in the simile-picture which is not paralleled in the actual episode, a detail put in, therefore, merely for the sake of completeness in the simile-picture. Now you will notice that the author by the use of this type of simile secures various desirable ends: first, he arrests attention by a sudden change of subject: next, by compelling his hearers to visualize two pictures at the same time, and to compare the details in the one with those in the other, he is keeping the imagination at full stretch; further, he is making it easier for his hearers to apprehend vividly, by this comparison of details, something which mere description could not render so vivid; the description, for example, of a man's state of mind is apt to be vague or dull, but compare it to the physical hunger of a lion and it immediately becomes clear; and lastly, I suggest as a further desirable end, which is often overlooked, that the poet by his simile gains *time* for his hearer. The simile-picture takes some time to draw, and during that time the hearer has leisure to grasp in full the other

[1] *Iliad*, iii. 21–37.

picture. Take the first simile of the third book in which the clamorous advance of the Trojans is compared in a five-line simile to the flight of cranes:[1] for the space of time which the five lines occupy in recitation the hearer is indeed seeing the cranes, but also, perhaps with another part of his mind, he is watching the Trojans advance. Without this, or some similar device, the poet can only say that the Trojans were advancing, and then, before the hearer has time to visualize the actual movement of the advance, the advance is finished and the hosts have met. And I think that often the irrelevant, or, perhaps better, superfluous, details are not used, as is frequently supposed, merely to give vividness to the simile-picture (though they do this too), but are used partly to give time, and are particularly common when the scene is of such a character (e.g. a scene of rapid and changing movement) that time is needed for its proper apprehension. When, for instance, in the sixteenth book of the *Iliad* we want time to watch the bustle and movement, as the Myrmidons arm at the order of Achilles, there is an eight-line simile comparing them to wolves.[2] But when the picture can be called up in its final form, when it is not necessary that it should change or develop under our eyes, when, for example, the armies, instead of advancing against one another, are locked in more or less static conflict, then two lines of simile about a man building a wall will suffice, or three about a boundary dispute or about a shipwright.[3]

But taking the similes as a whole, short or long, and granting that some of them have been displaced so that their applicability to the situation as we have it is either diminished or destroyed,[4] you will find, I think, that they either are, or in their original setting were, subservient to the main purpose, the vivid telling of a story. They are very seldom the mere exquisite interludes, the irrelevant though lovely adornments, which in a later type of epic they become. I quoted earlier Aristotle's comment on Homer as one who taught his followers ψευδῆ λέγειν ὡς δεῖ.

[1] *Iliad*, iii. 3–7. 'As the clangour of cranes rises to heaven, when they flee from winter and sudden rain-storms, and with clangour they fly to the streams of Ocean, bringing death and doom upon the Pygmy men, and deadly strife with the dawn.'
[2] *Iliad*, xvi, 156–63.
[3] *Iliad*, xvi. 212–13. *Ibid.* xii. 421–3. *Ibid.* xv. 410–12.
[4] Cf. G. Murray, *Rise of the Greek Epic*, pp. 215–18.

He is master and teacher of other things too, not least the simile, and he is its master, not its servant.

I said that these comparisons were to conclude the chapter. But a bald enumeration of Homeric qualities is no way to say farewell to Homer. May we end by seeing Homer at work; forget to analyse, and surrender to his power? I will put before you, out of many famous passages, one which presents Homer not at his grandest, but at his noblest and most human, and, as craftsman, most skilful. It is the farewell of Hector and Andromache. May I, at the possible cost of seeming an officious showman, but to avoid breaking the narrative, suggest in advance one or two points which may be worth notice: Homer's instinct which knows that Andromache, being Andromache, will forsake the merely personal appeal and, with pitifully vain tact, use the one argument which might sway her husband's judgement; Hector's tenderness for both his wife and his son, which yet cannot for an instant divert him from his implacable duty, nor prevent him from describing the hard fate that awaits her; the self-forgetful nobility of his prayer for the boy; the fact that even in their distress Hector and Andromache have not lost their sense of humour; and the skill with which for a few timeless moments the two great figures are isolated from the turmoil of war which surrounds them.

[Hector has gone home and not finding Andromache asks where she has gone. He is told that she has gone in haste and distress to the great tower, since she has heard that the Trojans are hard pressed and that there is a great strength of Achaeans against them.] 'And Hector rushed out of the house and made his way through the great city till he came to the Scaean gates, through which he would go out to the battle in the plain. And there Andromache met him, with the nurse carrying in her arms the baby, Hector's loved son, like a fair star. Hector's name for him was Scamandrios, but the rest called him "Prince of the City," for Hector alone was the saviour of Ilium. And he smiled as he looked in silence on the boy. And Andromache stood by him weeping, and she took his hand and spoke to him. "Hector, your great spirit will destroy you, and you have no pity for your boy or for me all ill-fated, who will so soon be your widow, for the Achaeans will set upon you all together and kill you. And when I am without you it were better for me to go beneath the earth, for there will be no comfort left me, but woes only. My kin are all dead . . . and you Hector alone are my father and mother, and my brother, and my strong lover. Have pity, and stay here on the tower, and do not make your child an orphan and your wife a widow. Draw up the people by the fig-tree, where the wall is most easy to scale and the city most open to attack. Three times already, just there, the best of the Greeks have made their assault, under the two Ajaxes, and famed Idomeneus, and the two sons of Atreus and the strong son of Tydeus."

'And Hector answered, "I have all that in my own mind, my dear. But I should be ashamed before all the men and women of Troy if I shrank from the war like a coward, and my own heart will not let me do it, since I have learned to stand with my people in the front rank of battle. Yet I know in my heart that the day will come when holy Ilium will go down in ruin, and Priam, and all the people of Priam. But all the agony of the Trojans, even of Hecuba and Priam and my brothers, who will fall in the dust at the hands of their foemen, is less to me than yours when some Achaean leads you away in tears, and the day of freedom is ended for you. And in Argos you will weave at another woman's loom, and bear water from the springs of that land, often ill treated and under hard thraldom. And a looker-on will say, as he sees you weeping, 'Hector's wife, she was; he was the best fighter of all the Trojans, when they were fighting round Ilium.' And your sorrow will be renewed, in the want of such a man who might have kept from you the days of slavery. But may the piled earth cover my dead body before I hear your cry as you are dragged off."

'So saying, Hector stretched out his arms for his son. But the boy shrank back with a cry into the bosom of his nurse, scared by the sight of his dear father, frightened by the bronze and the horse-hair plume, when he saw it nodding terribly from the helmet's crest. His father and mother laughed lovingly at him, and Hector took the helm from his head and set it down, all gleaming, on the ground, and then he took his son and kissed him and dandled him, and prayed to Zeus and the other gods. "Zeus, and you other gods, grant that this my son may be, as I have been, a chief among the Trojans, a good warrior and a strong ruler in Ilium. And may they say, as he comes back from

E

war, 'Here is a far better man than his father was.' And may he bring back with him the bloody arms of the foeman he has killed, so that his mother will be glad at heart."

'So saying he gave his son into the hands of his loved wife. And she took him to her fragrant bosom, smiling through her tears. And her husband pitied her as he watched, and he put his hand on her, and called her by name and said, "My dear, do not be over troubled for me, for no man shall send me down to Hades against the will of fate. No man ever yet has escaped his doom, brave man or coward, since the day that he was born. Go home now, and busy yourself with your own tasks, the loom and the distaff, and see that the maids busy themselves at theirs. And all the men of Troy will see to the war, and I the first among them."

'So Hector spoke, and took up again the crested helmet. And his dear wife went homewards, looking back as she went, and weeping.'[1]

[1] *Iliad*, vi. 390–496.

CHAPTER THREE

꙳ꙮꚝꚗꚞꚟ

LITERARY EPIC

HAVING NOW LOOKED AT SOME EXAMPLES OF ONE TYPE OF EPIC, let us examine the literary form which developed from it, the so-called 'literary' epic. Let me remind you first of the qualities which we found to be characteristic of the primitive epic. It is composed to be recited, not written to be read; its sole aim is to tell a story; this story deals with scenes familiar to both reciter and audience, and with the minute details of those scenes; and it deals with men and women just as men and women, 'doing and suffering'; everything in its technique is directed towards its one aim; it is rapid in movement; and literary adornment, such as simile, is either conspicuously absent, or, if present, is rigidly subordinated to the claims of the narrative.

Literary epic is something different; and something much more widely different than its name would suggest. Not only are its methods, for all their superficial resemblance, quite distinct, but by these distinct methods it aims at a different mark. The telling of a story is no longer the only, nor even the primary object; the story is a means to an end; the poem has an ulterior design upon us; the end may be patriotic or philosophic or ethical or theological, but it is something other than the plain straightforward delight of the reader in a moving story magnificently told. As a result the characters, not being of first-rate importance in themselves, are less clear cut, and are apt to degenerate either into mere types or even into mere symbols.

Compare the openings, superficially similar, of the *Odyssey* and the *Aeneid*. 'Tell me, Muse, of a man of many devices, and his far wanderings, and the many toils he suffered in seafaring, trying to win, for himself and his companions, life and a return to their own country.' It is an individual man that we are to hear about. Virgil starts (probably) with the prelude of four graceful lines, explaining his transition from pastoral to epic. Then he says he is to sing of arms and a hero who came by the decrees of fate from Troy to Italy, and suffered much on the sea and in war—so far much like the *Odyssey*; but then come the words 'until he should found a city and bring the gods to Latium, whence sprang the Latin race and the lofty walls of Rome.' And we are instantly aware, for all that it is slid in by a subordinate clause, that here is the real subject of the epic; it is not the fortunes of the wanderer, it is the founding of an empire. Or contrast the opening of the *Iliad* with that of *Paradise Lost*. 'Sing, goddess, of the wrath of Achilles Peleus' son, ruinous, which brought countless woes upon the Achaeans and sent many strong heroes down to Hades.' Again the subject is a man, and though the effects of his wrath extend beyond himself, it is upon other individual men that it brings destruction. But see what a difference in the opening of *Paradise Lost* the absence of an indefinite article can make. It is not of *a* man we are to read but of Man (generic), and of the effect of a transgression, not upon an individual, but upon humanity: and when later Milton states his purpose in explicit terms 'To justify the ways of God to men,' we know just how far we have moved from the spirit of the epic that wants to tell us of Achilles and Hector and Helen, of Odysseus and Penelope.

And if the spirits of the two types of epic are dissimilar, there is at least this difference in their circumstances. The literary epic is written to be read, to or by a cultivated circle of readers, who have probably little first-hand acquaintance with the scenes described. Detailed technical description will be not only unnecessary but tedious, and the writer can count upon a leisurely perusal, a sensibility in the reader for literary associations of language, and time for those associations to tell. Beauty of language is therefore no longer merely a means of enhancing the vividness of the narrative—this being in any case no longer of the first importance—nor even a means of enforcing the ulterior designs. It has become exalted into an end in itself.

Now when we come to examine the *Aeneid* as a typical
literary epic we are faced by the question at which I hinted
before. Is it either legitimate or useful to compare Virgil with
Homer, to use the term 'authentic' epic with the implication of
the damaging correlative 'spurious.' It is often said or implied
that any such comparison of Homer and Virgil is worse than
futile, that you might as profitably and justly compare the
Praxiteles Hermes and a Beethoven symphony, both being
great works of art in their kind, but from difference of kind not
directly comparable, so that any attempt at comparison
implies a confusion of thought. This sounds an attractive and
superior sort of critical doctrine, but it is worth considering
whether it is true. The truth appears to be this; both Homer
and Virgil are writing epic in the sense that both are writing
narrative poetry; Virgil may have another design, but he has
at least chosen narrative poetry as a means of accomplishing
his design. If on examination you find qualities in Homer which
Virgil lacks, and—the important proviso—*those qualities are
essential to narrative poetry*, then a comparison is valid and
damaging to Virgil. You may very rightly go on and find
qualities in Virgil which have nothing to do with narrative
poetry, and these will lie outside the scope of a comparison, and
will be estimated on their merits; but the discovery of these
qualities has nothing to do with the validity of a comparison of
the two writers as epic poets. One may illustrate the point in
another way. It would rightly be considered a waste of time to
compare Sophocles and Shakespeare, if our object were to
assign them places in a scale of merit, rather than to make an
interesting study in differences of method. But that is because
we do not regard the observance or neglect of the unities, nor
the presence or absence of a chorus, as essential features of
drama. If we did regard any of these as essential, then a
comparison would be valid, and damaging to one or other of
the dramatists. It may seem waste of time to labour this point,
but it seems to me a cardinal point in literary criticism, and one
over which there is considerable muddled thinking and
confusion of issues.

Now for any kind of story-telling, whether it is a child's
fairy tale or a great epic, we do demand certain qualities which
we find in Homer; reasonable rapidity; truth, in the sense that

the reader must never doubt the narrator's conviction, but must, if you like, be content to dream, with a willing suspension of disbelief; and characters clear-cut and in the round. In all these particulars Virgil is gravely deficient. He is seldom rapid, he is by no means always true, and most of his characters are little better than names or symbols.

He is not rapid. The Virgilian method of itself forbids rapidity. Virgil almost never draws with one bold stroke; he builds up his effects by touch on subtle touch. H. W. Garrod, in his acute preface to the Oxford Book of Latin Verse, described this method, perhaps rightly, as a particular type of the art of rhetoric (a practical art, which the Romans highly exalted), and he gives an illuminating example. Take another characteristic Virgilian passage:

> Nox erat, et placidum carpebant fessa soporem
> Corpora per terras, silvaeque et saeva quierant
> Aequora, dum medio volvuntur sidera lapsu,
> Cum tacet omnis ager, pecudes pictaeque volucres,
> Quaeque lacus late liquidos quaeque aspera dumis
> Rura tenent, somno positae sub nocte silenti.[1]

Now observe; *nox erat*, it was night. The remaining six lines add exactly nothing that is not implied in those words: 'all tired things were quietly slumbering throughout the earth'—watch the poet's imagination straying world-wide from the scene in hand; then we are raised above the earth, and look down on the sleeping woods and seas; lift your eyes and there is the silent wheel of the stars; then we sink to earth again, 'the country is silent, the beasts, the birds, are silent—both kinds of birds—sunk in sleep under'—here we are back again at our starting point—'the silent night.' Now we are for the moment, remember, criticizing this not as poetry, but as *epic* poetry. It is, I suppose one of the loveliest descriptions of night in literature ; the soft cadences are themselves an opiate to sink us Lethewards, and the man who wrote the lines had seen and felt for himself the peace of such a night. If you want to write nature poetry that is the way to do it—if you can. But it is no sort of way to tell a story. Indeed when the reader becomes acutely conscious of the technique, it is often actively exasperating. In this particular

[1] *Aeneid*, iv. 522–7.

instance, at a crisis in the fortunes of Dido, we want to know simply that it is night, and that Dido alone is awake in a sleeping world. That could have been told us in a line and a half. See how Homer does it:

δύσετό τ' ἠέλιος σκιόωντό τε πᾶσαι ἀγυιαί.[1]

Even when he takes more than a line over it, the phrasing is such that expectation is aroused:

ἄλλοι μέν ῥα θεοί τε καὶ ἀνέρες ἱπποκορυσταὶ
εὗδον παννύχιοι, (ἄλλοι μέν, so someone must be awake)
Δία δ' οὐκ ἔχε νήδυμος ὕπνος.[2]

We are at once alert, and inquisitive to know what it is that keeps Zeus from his bed.

Or observe the unconscionable time it takes Virgil to get a man killed; seven lines: 'So he spoke and towered above him with sword aloft and right between the temples he clove his forehead.' The man, one might suppose, is dead. But is Virgil content to let him be dead in peace and get on to the next victim? Not by five lines. We go on, 'his forehead and his boyish cheeks with the dreadful stroke. There was a crash and the earth shook with his mighty fall. His limbs relaxed and he lay there dying, his armour covered with blood and brains.'[3] It appears that by a miracle or a robust constitution he was not killed when his head was cloven and that even now he is not dead but only dying; but at least we have got him lying on the ground, though it has taken two and a half lines to get him there. But even yet Virgil is not finished with him, cannot give him the literary *coup de grace* without telling us all over again what we know already, that his head is cloven; 'and the two halves of his head hung one on this shoulder and one on that.' It is over at last and, in spite of all the blood and brains, how unconvincing it all is. Now it may equally take Homer six lines to get a man down, but the difference in method is complete. Each touch adds a new detail, and the picture is a moving picture. He never says the same thing twice, never goes back on his

---

[1] *Odyssey*, iii. 497. 'The sun sank, and all ways were shadowed.'
[2] *Iliad*, ii. 1. 2. 'All the other gods and plumed warriors slept nightlong, but sweet sleep had no hold upon Zeus.'
[3] *Aeneid*, ix. 749–55.

tracks. 'Odysseus' arrow took him in the neck, and the point
went clean through his throat, and he fell backwards, and the
cup slipped from his hand, and a stream of thick blood poured
from his nostrils, and he kicked the table from him and over-
threw it.'[1] And observe, lastly, how in Virgil the simile is
sometimes an end in itself. Take an instance in the sixth book.
Down in Hades a great crowd of shadows gathers to cross the
river to the Elysian plains, 'as at the first frosts of autumn
multitudes of leaves fall in the woods, or the hosts of birds
gather when the cold season of the year sends them fleeing over
the sea to sunny lands.'[2] It is an exquisite description; but you
will observe that in the first part the only appropriate feature of
the leaves is their number; that they are falling is irrelevant;
and in the second part the imagination ranges beyond what is
germane to the business and defeats its immediate ends; the
significant point is the gathering of the birds, but the imagination
follows them in their southward flight and so is distracted from
the shades on the bank. The touch is exquisite in itself, but it
mars the picture for its immediate purpose. Or if, with Sellar,
you defend it, and the defence is possible, by finding in the
terrae apricae a hint of the happier life beyond the barrier, then
consider this example. There is a comparison, in the fifth book,
of the Trojan youth, engaged in the complicated evolutions of
their military tattoo, first to the Labyrinth and secondly to
dolphins;[3] of these similes the first, one may safely say, is
thoroughly bad, since the rapidly shifting intricacies of the
horsemen are made not more but less vivid by comparison with
the static intricacies of the maze. And the second simile is
introduced merely in an attempt to remedy the deficiencies of
the first. Not all Virgilian similes are of this type; we shall
examine later one of exquisite perfection. But these and other
like examples are indications of the secondary importance which
is attached to vividness and continuity of actual narration.

The *Aeneid* is not true, except occasionally and as it were by
accident. The wanderings of Aeneas were as mythical and unreal
to Virgil as to his hearers, and many scenes and figures are there
not because they are interesting but because they are in the
Epic tradition. Consider for a moment the Gods and the battles.

---

[1] *Odyssey*, xxii. 15-20.   [2] *Aeneid*, vi. 309-12.
[3] *Aeneid*, v. 588-95.

Recall the gods in Homer. They may be disconcertingly unlike our notion of what gods should be; they are often more human than divine, and indeed a large part of their function is to provide the comic relief in the epic; but they are at least real and vividly real. And a few of them are a great deal more than merely amusing. Zeus, though he can unbend, and though he is hardly a pattern of virtue, is a great king, and Father of Gods and men. Poseidon is too strong and grim to be amusing, and Athene, though something of a shrew and excessively disputatious in the *Iliad*, has become in the *Odyssey* a stately and gracious figure. But whether the gods' function is to awe or to amuse they never fail to interest. They are an integral part of the action, as solid and familiar as the human actors. Now it is hardly an exaggeration to say that no one except perhaps a student of comparative mythology was ever yet interested in the gods of the *Aeneid*. They have no real existence; they are neither human nor divine, but merely a convention, a part of the epic machinery which in Virgil's day was obsolete. The gods indeed are so unfamiliar to the audience that they have to be elaborately introduced. Look at Mercury in Book IV. Hermes, we know, is the messenger of the gods and the merest passing reference to the winged sandals is enough. But here we have a passage which reads like an extract from a Classical Dictionary.[1] (If, of course, for the purposes of the succeeding scene it had been necessary that we should picture Mercury carrying the wand there would have been cause for the elaborate description of it; but there is no such justification.)

Or look at the battles. Virgil's descriptions are the merest conventional blood and thunder and have about as much verisimilitude as a stage fight. He barely knows the difference between a *hasta* and a *pilum*, and little it matters, since neither the poet nor his readers have the faintest shadow of interest in what he is talking about. So long as there is plenty of sound and fury and a deal of blood flowing and a respectable number of

[1] *Aeneid*, iv. 239–44. 'First he bound on his feet the golden winged sandals which carry him soaring high over sea and land with the speed of the winds. Then he took his wand: with this he calls spirits of the dead from Orcus and send others down to the gloom of Tartarus, and brings sleep or takes it away, and closes the eyes of the dying.'

corpses, honour—or tradition—is satisfied and there has been an epic battle. The typical lines are such as these:

> continuo adversis Tyrrhenus et acer Aconteus
> conixi incurrunt hastis primique ruinam
> dant sonitu ingentem perfractaque quadrupedantum
> pectora pectoribus rumpunt; excussus Aconteus
> fulminis in morem aut tormento ponderis acti
> praecipitat longe et vitam dispergit in auras.[1]

There is a great deal of crashing and clamour, but no real reason for Aconteus' meteorological demise. Or again, with slightly less inadequate detail to begin with and then taking refuge in the foggiest generalities,

> latos huic hasta per armos
> acta tremit duplicatque virum transfixa dolore.
> funditur ater ubique cruor; dant funera ferro
> certantes pulchramque petunt per vulnera mortem.[2]

It is all utterly unreal. Virgil is moving with fair grace, but with the weariness of complete indifference, through a series of conventional postures. But now watch the knowledgeable gusto with which Homer sets about a fight. 'Hector drew his sword and crouched and sprang; and Achilles met him'—Achilles' armour is described in detail—'and he balanced his spear in his right hand and he looked at Hector with death in his heart'

$$\epsilon i\sigma o\rho \acute{o}\omega \nu \; \chi\rho\acute{o}a \; \kappa a\lambda\acute{o}\nu, \; \acute{o}\pi\eta \; \epsilon\ddot{i}\xi\epsilon\iota\epsilon \; \mu\acute{a}\lambda\iota\sigma\tau a,$$[3]

'looking at his fair skin to judge where it would yield most easily. And the rest of him was covered with bronze, the glorious arms that he had stripped from Patróclus when he slew him; but there was one place exposed, where the collar-bone

---

[1] *Aeneid*, xi 612–17. 'Straightway with spears couched Tyrrhenus and fiery Aconteus charged each other, and the noise of their hurtling encounter rose high, and the breast-bones of their steeds were broken as they crashed together; Aconteus was hurled from his saddle in the fashion of a thunderbolt or a stone shot from a war-engine, and he fell headlong and his life was scattered to the winds.'

[2] *Aeneid*, xi, 644–7. 'Through his broad shoulders the spear drove its way, and stuck there, quivering, while the warrior, spitted, bent double in agony; dark blood streamed all around; locked in conflict they deal death with the steel, and seek the wounds that bring a noble end.' [3] *Iliad*, xxii. 321.

holds the shoulder from the neck, the gullet, where death most swiftly enters. There, as he rushed, Achilles drove at him with the spear, and the point went clean through his neck but without cutting the windpipe.' Here is a writer who knows every move in the game, and could, one fancies, play it himself if needed.

A minority of the Virgilian characters are in any proper sense alive. The great majority are hardly individuals at all; they are for the most part a scratch collection of supers merging indistinguishably into a common background from which the main figure should stand out. But the main figure entirely refuses to stand out from any background however drab. He is indeed the most impossible hero; for sheer soporific dullness he is without a rival, and the Arthur of Tennyson's *Idylls* is a vivid, warm-blooded human being beside him. We are not interested in him because Virgil was not; he was interested, and vitally interested, in something quite different, in the founding of Rome, in the Roman character, and in Roman antiquities. Aeneas is nothing more than a symbol of foundation, and an embodiment of Roman virtues, *pietas* the chief. I know that in our eyes Aeneas suffers more than is just from his stock epithet, which meant something so much nobler to the Romans than it does to us. But it is difficult to imagine that even a Roman—particularly if he were acquainted with heroes who were glancing-helmed or swift-footed—could have been much more stirred by a hero whose main characteristic was a perpetual *pietas* than we are by the 'blameless king.' For the greater part of the time Aeneas is too good for the human reader's imaginative food; one cannot say too bright, since that is perhaps the very last word one would think of applying to Aeneas. The unhappy hero finds the *moles* of founding Rome so oppressive that he passes across the stage in a settled gloom. When for a while he is not too good, as in the Dido episode, he becomes human at the cost of becoming also, by ordinary human standards, a mean scoundrel. Not all the characters are as stockish as Aeneas. When they are not hampered and harried by divine destinies they sometimes come alive. Turnus certainly does, though he loses by his frequent description as an abstract quality;[1] Nisus and Euryalus do, and so does Mezentius,

---

[1] 'violentia Turni.'

who, you observe, is significantly *contemptor divom*. And there is of course one complete exception to this weak individualization, the great queen of Carthage, who swept not only Aeneas but her creator temporarily off their feet. Dido is indeed a real and tragic figure; while she holds the stage, Troy is forgotten and the Roman empire no more than the small dust in the balance. We are carried away by the intensity of her passion and her anguish from the world of phantoms, where history is symbolized, to the world of life, where hearts are broken. But the moment of inspiration passes; Aeneas and Virgil both recover their balance; and one of the foundation stones of Rome is the betrayal of a queen. And we learn again how the artist is hampered by a purpose and a patriot by the artistic instinct.

Let me just put this question: What is it in Homer and Virgil that we remember? Out of those two treasure-houses what is it that we carry away with us for our permanent possession? Is it not in Homer men and women and whole scenes? Achilles chasing Hector, Thetis comforting her son, the greeting of the dog Argus, the slaying of the suitors, Achilles striding through the asphodel meadow of the world of shades and Ajax standing sullenly aloof and silent;[1] and are not even the memorable single lines connected in our memories with particular scenes or people? But is it not in Virgil lines and half-lines and short passages, often wholly unrelated to their context? For twenty readers who can tell you the occasion and the speaker of

νῦν δ' ἔμπης γὰρ κῆρες ἐφεστᾶσιν θανάτοιο,[2]

and know who stood

δακρυόεν γελάσασα,[3]

or, when they hear the great line

καὶ σέ, γέρον, τὸ πρὶν μὲν ἀκούομεν ὄλβιον εἶναι,[4]

can tell you who the old man was and why he was happy aforetime, will you find one who can tell you with certainty who

---

[1] *Iliad*, xxii. 134 onwards; *Iliad*, i. 357 onwards; *Odyssey*, xvii. 300–27; *Odyssey*, xxii; *Odyssey*, xi. 538–44.

[2] *Iliad*, xii. 326. 'But now, since the fates of death stand hard upon us.'　　　　[3] *Ibid*. vi. 484. 'smiling through her tears.'

[4] *Iliad*, xxiv. 543. 'Of you also, old man, we have heard that aforetime you were happy.'

it was that remembered Argos in his death[1] or of whose fate
it was that the gods ordained otherwise,[2] or when he quotes
sunt lacrimae rerum[3] can tell you the occasion and the full context
of that much-misused quotation? Yet this one reader can
probably quote you more lines of Virgil than all the twenty can
of Homer.

And this reflection brings us to the other side of the question.
I wonder how many readers have been accusing me of incon-
sistency who earlier described Virgil as a great poet and have
here been spending some time in exposing his deficiencies. I do
not plead guilty, for there are more kinds of poet than one. I
think that Virgil was a great poet of a particular kind, but that
he seems to have taken almost perverse trouble to obscure his
greatness under a bushel; indeed under several bushels, which
have to be successively removed before the light shines clear,
though when we come to it it is one of the most irradiating
lights in all literature. In the first place we have seen reason
to think that he was a very bad epic poet; literary epic in its
nature is liable to fall below primitive epic, but, as we shall
see when we come to *Paradise Lost*, there is no need to make it as
lifeless and tedious as Virgil made it. He was a considerable
antiquarian; and the alliance of antiquarianism and poetry is
usually a mésalliance; the Muse, in spite of language, refuses to
be domiciled in a Museum. Further, he was a patriotic Roman,
and it is typical of Rome that he willingly devoted, or, if you
like to put it more harshly, prostituted, his art to his patriotism.
He was a consciously and conscientiously patriotic poet, which
some would say is the same as being no poet at all.

So to find the true poet in Virgil we have to neglect him when
he is driving the epic car, for the machinery does little but creak
and groan, as is the way of second-hand machinery; and we
shall be wiser to stop our ears when he deliberately mounts the
patriotic rostrum, for he is then liable to a bad attack of
rhetoric; and we can safely go to sleep when he is engaged
upon antiquarian research. But when he is the poet of nature,
the philosopher poet, the poet of the human soul, then we are
inexcusable if we do not listen. And he is apt to put on his
singing robes with very little warning. Look for example at the

---

[1] *Aeneid*, x. 782: Antores.   [2] *Ibid.* ii. 428: Rhipeus.
[3] *Ibid.* i. 462.

descent into Hell, the one point perhaps where Virgil turned his
necessity to glorious gain. There was a νέκυια (a visit to the
shades) in Homer so the *Aeneid* must have one; but what a
different νέκυια! This is Plato, not Homer. And in the course of
it comes that great imaginative vision of the birth and growth
and being of the Universe, and the fate of human souls.[1] It has
no business at all in an epic; it intolerably delays the action;
but in itself it is one of the topmost peaks of Roman poetry and
one of the loftiest in the literature of the world.

And when you have accepted these reservations, when you
do not demand a story, and forget the ulterior patriotic object,
when you are content to concentrate upon those parts of the
poem which are lyric rather than epic, then you find the true
Virgil, the Wizard. In the first place, for consummate verbal
artistry he is probably unequalled; the tribute of the most
Virgilian of English poets to his great forerunner is not extravagant:

> All the chosen coin of fancy
> flashing out from many a golden phrase;
>
> All the charm of all the muses
> often flowering in a lonely word.[2]

I wish we had time to study his artistry in detail, to wander at
leisure through the flowered fields. I will give you just two
instances. One is the perfect simile that I earlier contracted to
show you, perfect in delicacy and appropriateness. Aeneas
catches a glimpse of Dido in the shades and is not sure that it is
she:

> agnovitque per umbras
> obscuram, qualem primo qui surgere mense
> aut videt aut vidisse putat per nubila lunam.[3]

The other is again a description of night:

> Ibant obscuri sola sub nocte per umbram
> perque domos Ditis vacuas et inania regna:

---

[1] *Aeneid*, vi. 724–51.   [2] Tennyson, *To Virgil*.
[3] *Aeneid*, vi. 452–4. 'He recognised her through the shadows, but
unsurely, as a man who sees, or thinks he has seen, the new moon
rising through cloud.'

quale per incertam lunam sub luce maligna
est iter in silvis, ubi caelum condidit umbra
Iuppiter, et rebus nox abstulit atra colorem.[1]

But, if a man is to be counted a great poet, he must have some
power more than that of mere verbal felicity. If it is at all a
definition of a great poet that he and he only has given full
and final expression to particular longings, aspirations, or
sorrows, of the human heart, that he and he only can securely
touch certain strings in the harp of human emotion, then
Virgil is beyond question one of the great poets of the world. He
is, beyond all others the poet of the pathos of two things, the
inevitable and the unattainable. Look at some of his favourite
epithets and some of his memorable phrases, *irrevocabile tempus,
ineluctabile fatum, quisque suos patimur manes,*[2] *stat sua cuique dies,*[2]
breve et irreparabile tempus; there rings through all of them the
helpless cry of humanity before the ordered march of the
universe. But if one were asked to give the most Virgilian line
that Virgil ever wrote one would hardly hesitate for the answer:

> Tendebantque manus ripae ulterioris amore.

He believes that man's reach not only should, but always must,
exceed his grasp; nor does he at all share Browning's confident
optimism that there is a heaven where Tantalus will grasp the
fruit.

We have now come to the last of our examples of epic, our
own great English literary epic, *Paradise Lost*.

Even a cursory comparison of *Paradise Lost* and the *Aeneid* will
suggest that in spite of similarities in technique there is one
fundamental difference; it is a difference typical of the races to
which the authors belonged. It is characteristic of Rome that
she subjugated even art to her own ends; she took a great poet
who, like others from across the Po, had much of 'the Celt' in
him, and bound him a willing slave to the triumphal progress
of her imperial chariot. Virgil knew as well as any man that

---

[1] *Ibid.* 268–72. 'They went darkling through the shades of the
lonely night, and through the empty abodes of Dis and his vacant
realms; as under the shifting light of the malignant moon there lies a
path through the woods, when Jupiter has hidden the heaven in
cloud, and black night has stolen all colour from the world.'

[2] 'each of us suffers his own hell.' *Aeneid*, vi.743. 'for each man
his day of fate is waiting.' *Aeneid*, x. 467.

there were greater things in life than the Roman Empire, that the human soul with its struggles and defeats would long outlast all temporal magnificence. Yet, at least in part, he subdued his genius to the service of a great, but largely materialistic, ideal. Explicit patriotism in art inevitably dooms it to transience. Milton was as great a patriot as Virgil. He was indeed one of the most fiercely and insularly patriotic of Englishmen. For sheer arrogance of patriotism you will find it hard to rival the possessive pronoun at the end of a famous sentence: 'God is decreeing to begin some new and great period in his Church, ev'n to the reforming of Reformation it self. What does he then but reveal Himself to his servants, and as his manner is, first to his English-men?'[1] There is a touch of that magnificent audacity about it which makes one catch one's breath at *sed victa Catoni*.[2] But though to the service of the country he so passionately and proudly loved Milton was prepared to devote twenty of the best years of his life, and, on the same altar, with cold-blooded courage, wittingly to sacrifice his eyesight, he was not prepared to sacrifice his art. No one could have written the *Aeneid* but a Roman poet, and it was as a citizen of Rome in the age of Augustus that Virgil wrote it. It may be, I think it is, true that no one but an Englishman of the seventeenth century could have written *Paradise Lost*. But it was not as an Englishman of that time that Milton wrote it, but as a man, a citizen of eternity. We may be, in practical affairs, provincial, insular, a nation of shopkeepers, any other derogatory appellation you choose to select; and in practical affairs we are in many ways like the Romans, though probably with more imagination than they. But I think we can claim without vanity that our great writers have been among the least limited and provincial in the world. They rise out of the enclosed valleys of age and language and country to join the Greeks in the region of the pure and untrammelled imagination, leaving the Romans far below.

We can at least claim for our literature the vastest subject among the epics of the world. Milton undertook a design beside which a ten-years war or the founding of an empire are

[1] *Areopagitica*.

[2] Lucan, *Pharsalia*, i. 128: Victrix causa deis placuit, sed victa Catoni. ('The gods chose the winning side, Cato the losers.')

trivialities; a design more grandiose in conception even than Dante's journey from Hell to Heaven. One is almost aghast at the audacity and secure consciousness of power which should propose to itself an epic subject of such sweeping grandeur as the creation and fall of the human race. The avowed object is the justification of God's ways to men, and though this may seem a trifle patronizing to God, it at least sets the limit to epic development. Milton's background is not the plains of Troy, nor the shores of the Mediterranean, nor the whole of the Northland, but the universe; and the figures which stand out from it are of transcendent stature, God and Satan, Death and Sin and Chaos.

Now it is clear that a writer who proposes such a subject to himself compels himself thereby to face certain grave difficulties. The most obvious, though not the most serious, is the mere vastness of the subject. Unless he can maintain an almost impossible level of dignity and power he will not only fail, but fail with ignominy. The descent from the sublime to the ridiculous is always fatally easy; but when you are climbing the last peak of the sublime, if you once slip out of your steps there is no recovery, no rope will hold you, and you plunge straight to destruction. This primary difficulty Milton almost completely surmounted, as we shall see when we come to examine his technique. The second difficulty is graver, and is partially insurmountable, so that it is no fault of Milton's that he failed to surmount it. This is the difficulty of maintaining the interest. In the ordinary epic or drama the characters, if they are to stir and hold our interest, must be human; they must have human passions and emotions, be liable to sin and failure. One of the elements of interest is, as a rule, the spectacle of a conflict, either between the hero and external forces, or between conflicting elements in the hero's own nature; or both types of conflict may be presented. (In practice the first type is more common in epic and the second in drama.) In any case the issue of the conflict must be doubtful. I do not mean that the reader must be in ignorance of the issue (else no great work could be read a second time, nor much Greek drama even for the first time), but the issue must be hidden from the characters themselves. Now consider for a moment the characters which any epic or drama on the subject of *Paradise Lost* must include. God, sinless and omnipotent, so that the one

F

conflict is impossible and the outcome of the other known by the
participants to be inevitable; the Son and the loyal angels, equally
sinless, and, if not omnipotent, at least fighting under the banner
of an omnipotent God; Adam and Eve, very far from omnipotent, so that one conflict can be made interesting, but, until
the fall, sinless, and so quite non-human and proportionately
dull. Everyone must have felt how from the moment that the
apple is eaten Adam and Eve come suddenly alive and are
sympathetic figures. There remain the fallen angels; they are
capable of all human emotions and weaknesses, so that the one
conflict is possible, and even in the case of the other it is clear
that, where the issue is foreknown, the forlorn hope, the
foredoomedly vanquished, can be made more inspiring figures
than the serenely certain victor. But it is clear that this mathe-
matical process of exhaustion brings us face to face with the
difficulty that theological presuppositions and artistic demands
are going to be incompatible. Milton's object is to justify the
ways of God to men; it is no part of the object to make any
of the rebel angels sympathetic, still less admirable, figures.
And yet the instinct of the artist will try to override the theo-
logian's protests and irresistibly urge him in this direction. The
dilemma is complete: the good characters cannot be made
interesting, nor the interesting characters good. And between
goodness and interest no artist will hesitate for a moment. It is
no wonder then that Milton failed where no one could have
succeeded. God, the Son, and Adam and Eve before the fall, are,
as most readers who are honest will admit, merely dull. But
Satan in the earlier books is a magnificent, clearly individualized
and overpowering figure.

How does Milton compare as an epic artist with Homer and
Virgil? Let us start by examining our general impressions, and
ask ourselves the question which we asked before; what is it
in Milton that we particularly remember? Is it individual lines
and short passages, or is it scenes and people? The answer will
surely be that it is both. It is lines like:

> Those other two equall'd with me in fate,
> So were I equall'd with them in renown,
> Blind Thamyris and blind Maeonides,
> And Tiresias and Phineus, prophets old.[1]

[1] *Paradise Lost*, iii. 33–6.

and others which we shall shortly examine; but it is also the
great debate in Hell, Satan on his throne of royal state, the
encounter of Sin and Death, the capture of Satan by Ithuriel
and Zephon. And the more detailed our examination becomes
the clearer grows the conviction that Milton is an incomparably
finer epic artist than Virgil (which does not mean necessarily
a greater poet) and that whether we rate him above or below
Homer depends largely upon which kind of epic we like. Let
us take some points of contrast.

Milton's style is much less rapid than Homer's, but not less
strong; and if it seldom attains, indeed seldom aims at, the
exquisitely tender cadences of Virgil, it can rise to greater
splendour. There never was a style more virile or more sure of
itself. There is nothing here, as there is in the Homeric hexameter, of the careless sweep of natural forces, sea or storm: it is
the finished, deliberate, and compact style of the conscious
artist. It has about it far more than Virgil's the inexorable
rhythm of the marching legions. Take one or two only of many
possible instances:

> Darken'd so, yet shone
> Above them all the Archangel: but his face
> Deep scars of thunder had intrench'd, and care
> Sat on his faded cheek, but under brows
> Of dauntless courage, and considerate pride
> Waiting revenge.[1]

or

> High on a throne of royal state, which far
> Outshone the wealth of Ormus and of Ind,
> Or where the gorgeous East with richest hand
> Showers on her kings barbaric pearl and gold,
> Satan exalted sat, by merit rais'd
> To that bad eminence.[2]

One knows that there is no escape from this

> unhurrying chase,
> And unperturbèd pace,
> Deliberate speed, majestic instancy.[3]

[1] *Paradise Lost*, i. 599–604.   [2] *Paradise Lost*, ii. 1–6.
[3] Francis Thompson, *The Hound of Heaven*.

I do not think you will find in all Homer and Virgil any lines which can be compared to these for solemn, almost sombre, magnificence of music. It is doubtful whether you will find such music in any classical author except one, and that one Lucretius. And it is perhaps significant that both writers were strongly moved by a great and timeless subject.

In the second place, as a narrator Milton is indeed below Homer, but immeasurably above Virgil. His story may not move rapidly, but he is at least entirely possessed by the truth of it. Again I mean the essential truth. Milton no doubt would not have held as an article of faith the exact description of Satan's shield, still less the invention of gunpowder by the rebel angels: but in his story as a whole, the coming of sin and death into the world, man's fall and redemption, he believed with the full force of a strong and passionate nature. Hence while Virgil is perpetually losing his hold upon us, since you cannot transfer to a reader a conviction which you do not yourself possess, Milton never loses grip, except when he becomes deliberately and perversely tedious. And if the story does not move rapidly, it does at least move, maintaining for the most part a steady and indeed relentless progress. With Virgil we are often becalmed, as idle as a painted ship upon a painted ocean; then comes a breath of life, the sails fill, the sheets tauten, and the ship gathers way, only to miss stays completely at the next tack, or be again hopelessly becalmed. But there is none of this uncertainty with Milton. If his progress ceases it is because he has deliberately called a halt; and the halt, inartistic though it may be, is as fully intended as the disciplined and ordered march. If, however, you compare Milton with Homer, you will find that it is largely in these halts that his epic inferiority lies. He can on occasion rise above Homer, but he has not the latter's unflagging power, nor is his grandeur so well sustained. On this subject of the sustained grandeur of *Paradise Lost*, there is I think a great deal of cant commonly talked, largely by critics who are afraid that honesty will be an admission of incapacity. After reading much undiscriminating eulogy of this kind, and observing in particular Mark Pattison's intellectually snobbish remarks about the last reward of consummated scholarship, it is refreshing to turn to Johnson, declaring with his usual sound sense and honesty that no one ever wished *Paradise Lost* longer than it is. If we are thoroughly honest with ourselves, is not our verdict on *Paradise Lost* something like this?—that the first two books are almost beyond criticism, almost superhuman, in their intensity, compression, and power; that the war in Heaven rises to almost the same level; that in other books there are passages, often long passages, little if at all inferior, notably the opening of the third book and the close of the twelfth; that in the later books, though there is less magnificence, there is much exquisitely lovely writing; but that much of the later books is frankly tedious, and the interminable discourses of the affable archangel, coming as they do at a crisis of the action, quite intolerable?

Finally, as against Virgil, Milton can draw living characters. It is true that his failure is most complete where success, though indeed most difficult, was also for his purpose most important. It appears that there were two ways in which the presentation of God might have been attempted. The writer might have withdrawn Him altogether into the light unapproachable, and relied upon an impression of unseen but overwhelming power; or he might have been as wholeheartedly anthropomorphic as a Blake drawing, and described God with the utmost particularity of royal splendour. But Milton wavers between the two methods, and in the upshot God is no better than an arbitrary tyrant, vaguely drawn, who, so far as he is discernible at all, evokes little but contempt. Milton may justify God's ways to men, but the ways of the Miltonic God in general and towards Satan in particular are beyond hope of justification. But if we omit God, and the Son, who is only a degree or two less unsatisfactory, in the rest of his character delineation Milton is triumphantly successful. And the triumph is the more signal because of its difficulty. Milton contrives to differentiate his characters one from the other, and to make them vivid, without descending to a triviality of detail that would detract from their gigantic stature. See how clearly the dreadless angel is depicted; what a contrast between the warrior Gabriel and the communicative Raphael; how clearly in the great debate in Hell the characters of the disputants emerge from their speeches. Above all take Satan. He stands by the phantoms of the *Aeneid* as Odysseus among the strengthless dead; and even the great warriors of the *Iliad* are puny beside him, meriting little more than that small infantry warred on by cranes. But for all his superhuman greatness, the earlier Satan is such a magnificent epic figure because all his passions and emotions, to whatever pitch of intensity they are raised, are still the emotions and passions of humanity. His pride may be terrifying in its arrogance, and his tears such as angels weep, but they are yet the same pride and the same tears as those of men. Milton, like Virgil, was swept off his feet by his own creation, but he did not recover his balance with such apathetic ease. The Englishman was a greater artist than the Roman. As he would not sacrifice his art to his patriotism, neither would he sacrifice it to his theology. In the early books he concentrated interest where it was certain to ruin his design, just because in Satan, and in Satan only, was it possible from the artistic point of view that interest should be concentrated. There were doubtless other impulses which urged in the same direction. Milton was by temperament a rebel, and the appeal to him of the first and greatest rebel was no doubt irresistible. But it was the dominance in Milton of the artistic instinct over any other instinct or purpose whatsoever that made the epic what it is. Both Milton and Virgil found themselves trying to serve two masters: a choice was inevitable; and I think we may say that Milton's choice was the right one.

In all the respects in which Milton stands out as Virgil's superior, in style, in rapidity, in truth of narration, in character delineation, he comes closer to Homer. And yet the whole impression of his work is different. Why is this? There are, I think, two main reasons. In the first place, Homer, finished artist though he is, is telling a story for an audience of simple men, and his finished artistry is a finished simplicity and naiveté. Milton is not a more perfect artist, but he is a far more elaborate one. To him what one may call the purely literary aspect of his great work was of high importance. He had before him the two great epics of antiquity, and in large measure he combined their qualities. In the greatest books of *Paradise Lost* there is much of the primitive epic spirit, but to enhance the general effect Milton has used all the resources of the literary epic; and in the furnace of his genius he has fused the two discordant elements into one harmonious and transcendent whole. Milton, like Virgil, is writing not for a simple but for a highly cultivated and sensitive audience, and he plays with consummate skill upon their culture and sensitiveness. He has all the resources of classical mythology and of Jewish myth and history on which to draw for the diversification and embroidery of his epic. And so he can employ with Virgil a literary artifice from which Homer was debarred even had he wished to use it; he can quicken his readers' imagination directly by the force or beauty of his descriptions; but he can exert a secondary and very delicately piquant appeal by the stirring of literary reminiscence. He is a slow, deliberate craftsman and the result of his labours is work of unsurpassed richness, the reddest of gold overlaid and encrusted with all manner of precious stones, and as the light falls on them it is reflected from one to the other in bewilderingly intricate scintillations. Let us just take a few instances of this added richness which reminiscence gives: it may be nothing more than a classical turn of phrase or the classical use of a word (it is of course a commonplace that without some knowledge of Latin Milton is often barely comprehensible), as 'horrid hair,' or the Virgilian transferred epithet 'horizontal misty air,' or 'Adam the goodliest man of men since born', all which are little more than the natural mannerisms of a man to whom Latin and Greek were familiar languages; but take two instances already quoted: 'That small infantry warred on by cranes';[1] unless we know the relevant passage in Homer the word 'that' is meaningless; if we do, we have before our minds the picture of another great host. Or take the characteristic Miltonic simile of the elves which some belated peasant sees or dreams he sees.[2] This is vivid enough in itself and beautiful. It does not depend for its appeal on reminiscence: but if we remember the Virgilian parallel[3] and its context, the appeal is immeasurably heightened by its two-fold complication.

And while we are on the subject of the simile it is worth spending a few minutes in examining Milton's use of it. He has three distinct modes. The Homeric, the super-Virgilian, and one peculiar to himself, the negative.

[1] *Paradise Lost*, i. 575–6.   [2] *Paradise Lost*, i. 781–8.
[3] *See* p. 66 above.

The 'negative simile' (often not strictly a 'simile') is too well known to need illustration: it is an effective device, used to give at frequent intervals the impression of superhuman size and magnificence, and it has the merit that it avoids the necessity for direct description of the indescribable.[1]

Here is the Homeric:

> up they sprung
> Upon the wing, as when men wont to watch
> On duty, sleeping found by whom they dread,
> Rouse and bestir themselves ere well awake.[2]

Or at greater length, but still completely relevant, point for point:

> As when the potent rod
> Of Amram's song in Egypt's evil day
> Wav'd round the coast, up call'd a pitchy cloud
> Of locusts, warping on the eastern wind,
> That o'er the realm of impious Pharaoh hung
> Like Night, and darken'd all the land of Nile;
> So numberless were those bad angels seen
> Hovering on wing under the cope of Hell
> 'Twixt upper, nether, and surrounding fires;
> Till, at a signal giv'n, the uplifted spear
> Of their great Sultan waving to direct
> Their course, in even balance down they light.[3]

Or the comparison in Book II of Satan to a tiger 'who by chance hath spied In some purlieu two gentle fawns at play.'

Look lastly at this example of what I have called the super-Virgilian. The simile is not used only to make more vivid the actual scene or episode described: rather the scene or episode is the occasion for the introduction of a vivid but largely irrelevant picture:

> Angel forms, who lay entranc'd
> Thick as autumnal leaves that strow the brooks

[1] e.g. *Paradise Lost*, i. 717–19.

> Not Babylon,
> Nor great Alcairo such magnificence
> Equall'd in all their glories.

or *Paradise Lost*, iv. 268–85.

> Not that fair field . . .

[2] *Paradise Lost*, i. 331–4.   [3] *Ibid*. 338–49.

> In Vallombrosa, where the Etrurian shades
> High overarch'd embower; or scatter'd sedge
> Afloat, when with fierce winds Orion arm'd
> Hath vex'd the Red-Sea coast, whose waves o'erthrew
> Busiris and his Memphian chivalry,
> While with perfidious hatred they pursu'd
> The sojourners of Goshen, who beheld
> From the safe shore their floating carcases
> And broken chariot wheels.[1]

The autumn leaves are probably a reminiscence of the *lapsa cadunt folia frigore primo*,[2] though more fully appropriate; since they are strewing the brooks, as the angel forms the burning marle: the value of Vallombrosa and the Etrurian shades, however, is purely a sound value, a literary—or, if you like, musical—device: we then pass to sedge floating, and then some curious things happen: at the mention of the Red Sea the historical imagination is kindled, and sees the ruin of the Egyptians, allusively described, which comes in at first merely as an elaboration, and then by unobtrusive degrees becomes another simile on its own account.

And if Milton is a master in the use of simile of all types, he is also a master of the use of proper names in a way peculiar to himself. This is nothing but pure literary artifice. You find something remotely like it in Homer's stock epithets: and both Virgil and Homer occasionally have a line or two consisting of the names of indiscriminate nymphs or casualties. But neither of them ever, like Milton, plays a kind of fantasia upon proper names. One is almost weary of hearing of the organ voice of Milton, but the comparison is a just one, and when Milton is improvising upon proper names you are conscious of the fingers of the great player sliding from one reverberating or delicate chord to the next. Listen to the harmonies:

> in Hesebon
> And Horonaim, Seon's realm, beyond
> The flowery vale of Sibma clad with vines,
> And Eleale to the Asphaltic pool.[3]

> And all who since, baptiz'd or infidel,

---

[1] *Paradise Lost*, i. 301–11.   [2] *See* p. 60 above.
[3] *Paradise Lost*, i. 408–11.

> Jousted in Aspramont or Montalban,
> Damasco, or Marocco, or Trebisond[1]

> knights of Logres, or of Lyones,
> Lancelot or Pelleas, or Pellenore.[2]

> Blind Thamyris and blind Maeonides,
> And Tiresias and Phineus, prophets old.[3]

If any of you are interested in the fascinating study of the subtler intricacies of verbal music, may I commend any one of those passages to your attention? There are those who will tell you that such study of the technicalities ruins true aesthetic appreciation. Lord Balfour, in a famous Romanes Lecture, cogently expressed the contrary opinion. It is true that such study is ancillary only, but no one needs to be ashamed of an affection for it, and one returns from it with a clearer perception and quickened appreciation of the artistic beauty of the whole. If the study does no more than make you read a passage with your ears open,[4] it has done something for you. In the second passage for instance look at the way in which 'Montalban' repeats in the reverse order the entire last syllable and the vowels of the other two syllables of the preceding word: notice the effect of the repeated staccato short a, and the way in which the z and d of 'baptiz'd' are sharpened to s and t, and then blunted again for their repetition in the closing name of the passage. In the last passage listen to the effect of the reiterated long i, and the way in which (this is a favourite Miltonic trick[5]) the word 'prophets' picks up, and concentrates in one word, sounds which have occurred in separate predecessors.

[1] *Paradise Lost*, i. 582–4.   [2] *Paradise Regained*, ii. 360, 1.
[3] *Paradise Lost*, iii. 35–6.

[4] And incidentally your eyes shut: printed English is a deceptive language, and even to the native, let alone the unhappy foreigner, letters are not always what they seem. In the second passage above, for example, the c of 'Damasco' is what it appears to be, but the c is a k, while the s of 'Trebisond' is a z in masquerade, and the c of 'since' nothing but one of Tennyson's geese disguised.

[5] Cf. e.g. *Comus*, 116. 'Now to the moon in wavering morrice move,' where the last word picks up the m, v, and oo of the preceding words.

But the difference between Milton and Homer is more than
a difference of technique. We are conscious, I think, of a
dissimilarity much more fundamental, and one which sets
Milton further from Homer than from Virgil. However much
at times, and particularly with regard to the central figure of
his epic, Milton's art overcomes his purpose, he never forgets
his purpose. He is always deeply conscious of the profound
significance of his story. Homer is vividly conscious of the
interest of his story, but that is a different matter. Milton is
narrating something which has affected the destinies of the
whole human race, and this gives to his presentation a gravity
and weight of utterance which you will not find in the earlier
writer, whose story is all in the past, and has no implications for
the present. I put it to you (if I may borrow the language of the
Courts) that what fundamentally differentiates Milton is a
profound moral earnestness. I said earlier that *Paradise Lost*
could hardly have been written but by an Englishman of the
seventeenth century. Of the seventeenth century, because of
the particular theological colour: why by an Englishman? I
want to suggest to you that this quality which I have called
moral earnestness is characteristic of many of our writers, and
indeed, for all the reluctance with which it would admit the
notion, characteristic of our race as a whole, as also it was
characteristic of the Romans. I do not of course mean that our
great writers spend their time robing their art in an ill-fitting
surplice, and setting it to pound the cushion in the ineffective
pulpit of didacticism. I mean something more like a deep-
rooted consciousness of a 'moral order' in the world, and of the
absolute and permanent value of goodness. Shakespeare, for
example, is at once the least and most moral of dramatists. The
copybook moralist or the writer of tracts, though he can find
plenty of moral 'tags' scattered through the plays, would be
hard put to it to discover what is ordinarily called a 'moral' in
any Shakespearean drama: but there is no dramatist who gives
a clearer impression of the difference between right and wrong,
good and bad. Shakespeare knew as well as anyone that the
wicked frequently flourish like the green bay tree; but he was
equally sure that they are the wicked, and no amount of
flourishing can change that: and though he was aware of a soul
of goodness in things evil, he was vividly aware that there was

such a thing as evil, not to be confounded with good. And I
think you will find this same attitude of mind permeating the
great bulk of our literature. You get it, for example, at the end
of a comparatively light lyric:

> Only the actions of the just
> Smell sweet and blossom in their dust.[1]

or in an even lighter one:

> I could not love thee, dear, so much,
> Lov'd I not honour more.[2]

Even the conventional and trifling philosophizings of Herrick
have a touch of it. It is I think a savage and distorted form of it
which gives to Wycherley his peculiar flavour. Johnson, perhaps
the most typically English in strength and weakness of all our
great men of letters (and not the less an Englishman because
you feel him to be greater as a man than as a man of letters), is
directed and even warped by it: his outstanding quality as a
critic is a passion for sincerity, a moral quality: and his onslaught on *Lycidas*, wildly mistaken though we may think it, is a
moral rather than a literary judgement. In the typical, old-
fashioned melodrama, now unhappily defunct, it is not merely
the happy ending that must be secured, but a happy ending in
which the distinction between good and bad is emphasized,
however falsely, by their respective rewards. Dickens has this
attitude in its melodramatic, Scott and Fielding in its Shakespearean, form. But of all our writers there is no one who is so
completely informed by this temper of mind as Milton. And it
is because of this that his only true companion in poetry is one
of the most intense and most sublime of writers, whom the
limits of our subject unhappily exclude. Dante alone has the
same terrible power, the volcanic fire from the very centre of
things. They are σπουδαιότατοι τῶν ποιήτων.

---

[1] Shirley, *O.B.E.V.* 288.   [2] Lovelace, *O.B.E.V.* 343.

꧁꧂

CHAPTER FOUR

LYRIC

HUMANITY MAKES A VARIETY OF DEMANDS UPON ITS ARTISTS, upon those who express it to itself, giving articulate permanence to its half-articulate emotions. Narrative poetry satisfies one demand, and can be used for a diversity of ends; and drama satisfies another. But in answer to a different demand there arises inevitably another type of poetry which may be called occasional or personal, the direct expression of men's feelings in all phases and circumstances of human life, whether they are philosophizing or moralizing, or, more often, falling in love or out of it, mourning for the dead, preparing for war, or getting drunk. It has been generally agreed to call this type of poetry lyric. One need not spend time in considering how real a distinction this label implies. It may mean no more than that in this type of poetry the poet speaks in the first person. It may represent, as I think it does, a more fundamental distinction. But for the immediate purpose it will be sufficient to agree that lyric is an expression, usually brief, of a personal feeling, whether that feeling is a transient emotional mood such as the excitement of a revel, or of a long-continued emotional experience such as love of country. And since lyric is so all-embracing in its range and so personal in its expression, it follows that from lyric more than from any other form of literature we secure an insight into a nation's temper and its attitude towards life.

It is clear that for a form of poetry which is to include many poems both brief and intense the hexameter metre is unsuitable. Its sweeping movement requires space in which to deploy, and there is inevitably a certain absence of 'form' in any succession of hexameter lines, as there is in any ordinary succession of lines of English blank verse. The four lines of the famous fragment of Alcman which I instanced earlier[1] are purely lyric in spirit, but in the reading even of these there is, I think, a certain sense of dissatisfaction because they do not so much end as stop. The object of lyric is not to carry us on from point to point of a narrative, but to awaken in us the keenest possible realization of an emotion, 'stabbing the spirit broad awake'; and it is therefore a gain if the ear as well as the mind is aware of a satisfying arrest. We demand that the lyric music should end on a recognizably final chord, and not behave like the music of musical chairs. Further, since the emotional range of the lyric is so wide, the lyric writer must have ready to his hand a variety of metres. So the inventive Greek mind set to work and produced a wealth of new metres, the elegiac (nearest to the hexameter), iambic (nearest to ordinary prose), trochaic, anapaestic, choriambic, alcaic, sapphic, not to mention all the regularly irregular metres of the choric odes.

Equipped then with these diverse metres, and stimulated by a variety of emotions other than the traditional *rabies* of Archilochus, what kind of lyric did the Greeks produce? We are perpetually being told that the Greeks were lovers of beauty, which is no doubt true; but because to us a love of beauty means very largely love of beauty in nature, we expect to find the Greek love of beauty expressing itself in a wealth of exquisite nature lyric. When we fail to find the expected profusion, we are a little apt to run to the other extreme and assert that the Greeks were not nature-lovers at all, supporting the contention by reference to their limited sense of colour, or saying with Chesterton that they could not see the wood for the dryads. Now when we descend from a general impression to the particular examination of the Greek lyric it is no longer possible to maintain that the Greeks could not at any rate write lyrics about nature. We find ourselves faced with Alcman's description of night[2]

---

[1] *See* p. 11.
[2] (*O.B.G.V.* 117)

εὕδουσιν δ'ὀρέων κορυφαί τε καὶ φάραγγες,
πρώονές τε καὶ χαράδραι

('They are all sleeping, the peaks and the gorges of the mountains, the jutting crags and the ravines.')

(though it is true that most of the passage is little more than a catalogue), or by Sappho's description of the stars and the moon,[1] or the exquisite description of the coming of spring attributed to Meleager, or the list of flowers in Heliodora's garland, much like the list in Shelley's *The Question*.[2] Nevertheless the number of extant Greek nature lyrics is comparatively small; and, even in those that we have, this peculiarity is, I think, observable; except in the Sicilian Theocritus you will search long in Greek lyric, or for that matter in Greek poetry at all, before you find any *affection* for nature as we understand the term; and still longer before you find that imaginative attitude, so familiar to us, which attributes personality to natural objects. The absence of the note of affection is natural enough. The Greeks, or at any rate the literature-producing Greeks, were on the whole a nation of town-dwellers; their state is the city-state; and their qualities are all those which are fostered by life in a society, versatility, intellectual keenness, and that eagerness for affairs which was apt to degenerate into 'busy-bodyness.' Philosophers might bestow theoretic praise upon the 'contemplative life,' the θεωρητίκος βίος; but to the ordinary Greek a 'wise passiveness' would have been a contradiction in terms, an attitude not wise but foolish and characteristic of the contemptible ἰδιώτης;[3] and, as is usual with the sensitive town-dweller, the Greek's attitude towards nature is an attitude towards something lovely, stirring in him perhaps a keen sense of beauty, but something external and alien, towards which he cannot feel any human emotion. In nothing is Keats more characteristically Greek than in his attitude towards the nightingale. As the swallow of the famous 'Swallow Song'[4] is no more than a signal, so to Keats the nightingale is not so much a sentient being, a small brown bird with its own domesticities,

[1] (*O.B.G.V.* 142)

> ἄστερες μὲν ἀμφὶ κάλαν σελάνναν
> ἂψ ἀποκρύπτοισι φάεννον εἶδος,
> ὅπποτα πλήθοισα μάλιστα λάμπῃ
> γᾶν ἐπὶ παῖσαν

'Stars round the lovely moon hide their shining beauty when she lightens the earth with the full tide of her brightness.'

[2] *O.B.G.V.* 580, 581.

[3] The 'private' man, who wants to 'live his own life' and not concern himself with the affairs of the city.   [4] *O.B.G.V.* 130.

for which affection or pity might be felt, as something—it matters little whether sentient or not—which by its song rouses him to a rapture of ecstatic emotion. To that emotion he gave unrivalled expression—the *Ode to a Nightingale* is beyond dispute one of the chief jewels in the regalia of English poetry—but it is surprising, if one has not studied it from that point of view, to find, on re-reading that lovely and justly famous poem, how little there is in it about its ostensible subject.

As to the second point, it may have appeared absurd to suggest that the Greeks had little sense of personality in nature, when one remembers the naiads, and the dryads, and the oreads. But that is precisely the point. The clear-cutting Greek mind saw the fountain or the hill as one thing, the naiad or the oread as quite another thing. If one imagines a being dwelling in a fountain it is just because one does not think of the fountain as a being in itself. To put it in another way, 'the spirit of the hills' implies an entirely different set of conceptions from 'the Spirit of Helvellyn.' Take a concrete instance, which has nothing to do with dryads, but illustrates much of the difference; here are the famous lines of Sappho about the last apple:

οἶον τὸ γλυκύμαλον ἐρεύθεται ἄκρῳ ἐπ' ὕσδῳ,
ἄκρον ἐπ' ἀκροτάτῳ· λελάθοντο δὲ μαλοδρόπηες,
οὐ μὰν ἐκλελάθοντ', ἀλλ' οὐκ ἐδύναντ' ἐπίκεσθαι.[1]

That is all perfectly clear and perfectly straightforward: the apple is an apple: and it is a nuisance to the apple-gatherers that they cannot reach it, but a matter of complete indifference to the apple. It, being an apple, cannot either want or not want to be gathered. Here, on the other hand, is Coleridge on the last leaf:

> There is not wind enough to twirl
> The one red leaf, the last of its clan,
> That dances as often as dance it can . . .[2]

And if this attitude differentiates the Greek nature lyric from our own, or, as I hope to show later, from that of the Romans, there is a comparable, though not identical, difference in the

[1] *O.B.G.V.* 148. 'As the sweet apple shines red on the high branch, at the very tip of the highest, and the apple-pickers have forgotten it —well, not forgotten, but they could not manage to reach it.'
[2] *Christabel*, I. 50.

lyrics of patriotism and war. No State in history has evoked a
patriotism more passionate than the city of the rocks and the
violet crown, whose citizens were her lovers; and the patriotism
of her great rival, though less fiery, was no less deep. But
whereas Roman and English patriotism has its roots deep in the
soil and demands something concrete to attach itself to, the
Greeks, like the French, found it easy not only to feel a devotion
to an abstract ideal but also to express that devotion in abstract
terms. One sees this in that lofty expression of patriotism which
we know as the funeral oration of Pericles; it is magnificent, but
it is only by an effort of the imagination that we allow ourselves
really to be moved by it; we do not easily breathe that rarefied
air. And the same is true of the Greek lyric. Take three famous
epitaphs, on the Spartans at Thermopylae, on the Athenians and
on the Spartans at Plataea:[1]

> ὦ ξεῖν’, ἀγγέλλειν Λακεδαιμονίοις ὅτι τῇδε
> κείμεθα, τοῖς κείνων ῥήμασι πειθόμενοι.

(We kept the Spartan law—O passer-by,
　So let the Spartans know—and here we lie.)

> εἰ τὸ καλῶς θνῄσκειν ἀρετῆς μέρος ἐστὶ μέγιστον
> ἡμῖν ἐκ πάντων τοῦτ’ ἀπένειμε τύχη·
> Ἑλλάδι γὰρ σπεύδοντες ἐλευθερίην περιθεῖναι
> κείμεθ’ ἀγηράντῳ χρώμενοι εὐλογίῃ

(If noble death is valour’s choicest crown,
　Fortune of all her gifts gave us the best;
We strove to give Greece freedom, and renown
　Is ours for ever as we lie at rest.)

> ἄσβεστον κλέος οἵδε φίλῃ περὶ πατρίδι θέντες
> κυάνεον θανάτου ἀμφεβάλοντο νέφος·
> οὐ δὲ τεθνᾶσι θανόντες, ἐπεὶ σφ’ ἀρετὴ καθύπερθεν
> κυδαίνουσ’ ἀνάγει δώματος ἐξ Ἀΐδεω

(Robing their land in fame that never fades
　These wrapped about them death’s dark cloud
　　of night;
But they in death are not dead; from the shades
　Their valour leads them honoured up to light.)

[1] *O.B.G.V.* 212, 214.

G

Observe how full they all are of abstractions, law, freedom, renown, fame, valour, and the like, and with what a sense of surprise we light upon the exception, as in that lovely epitaph on the Eretrians who fell in Media:

οἵδε ποτ' Αἰγαίοιο βαρύβρομον οἶδμα λιπόντες
'Εκβατάνων πεδίῳ κείμεθ' ἐνὶ μεσάτῳ·
χαῖρε, κλυτή ποτε πατρὶς 'Ερέτρια· χαίρετ', 'Αθῆναι
γείτονες Εὐβοίης· χαῖρε, θάλασσα φίλη.[1]

It would be absurd to fancy that such patriotism, stirred by abstractions and expressing itself in abstract terms, is either stronger or less strong than one which talks less easily of κλέος (glory) or *liberté*; but it is the patriotism of a different national temperament. The Roman and the English mind do not work in that way. What brought the homeward-bound Athenian's heart into his mouth was the sunlight on the spear-point of the statue of a goddess; to the returning English exile, before he returned by air, it was the Channel lights and the Dover cliffs; and I wonder whether it is an allegorical statue or one of the most superb sky-lines in the world, the block of buildings on the Battery, that tells the sea-borne American that he is home again.

I shall do no more than mention some other types of Greek lyric (if indeed they should properly be called lyric at all), the political-moralizing type of Solon and Theognis,[2] the bluntness of (perhaps pseudo-) Hipponax,[3] the reflections upon human nature of which Semonides' ungallant estimate of women[4] is an example. I cannot even do more than call passing attention to the famous σκόλια or drinking songs: in this class we find the light gay lyrics of Anacreon, whose potations from his own account seem—as usual with the Greeks—to have had a good deal of allaying Cayster in them; or the more satisfactory song of Hybrias; or the most famous of all, the 'Harmodius and Aristogeiton' song.

[1] *O.B.G.V.* 443.
> Here now we lie in midmost Media, we
>> Who left far off the Aegean's thundering swell;
>> Farewell, our glorious homeland; fare you well,
> Athens, our neighbour; and farewell, dear sea.

[2] e.g. *O.B.G.V.* 159, 185.   [3] *O.B.G.V.* 182.   [4] *O.B.G.V.* 122.

ἐν μύρτου κλαδὶ τὸ ξίφος φορήσω,
ὥσπερ Ἁρμόδιος καὶ Ἀριστογείτων,
ὅτε τὸν τύραννον κτανέτην
ἰσονόμους τ' Ἀθήνας ἐποιησάτην.[1]

(In myrtle wreathed I'll bear my blade
As did the famous twain
Who slew the tyrant, and so made
Athens free again.)

May I just ask you to keep in mind the general impression of
the Greek drinking songs, since we shall come back to them,
and let us go on to look at the two great figures in Greek lyric.
They are the figures of the Watts picture, but with a clarity of
outline of which that beautiful colourist and somewhat woolly
allegorist was seldom capable, Love and Death. It is when
dealing with these two that Greek lyric rises to its heights.

The poets who lived in a fighting age had a first-hand
acquaintance with violent death, and they do not blink the
horror of it; the laboured realism of many of the modern
poets of war is less unsparing than the quiet grimness of
Tyrtaeus' description of the old man dying in battle;[2] but
against this the Greeks set the glory of an honourable death;
and for the most part they were more concerned with the fact of
death than with its circumstances. The dead pass into a shadowy
world of which we know nothing. All that remains is their
work, or the remembrance of their valour. Heracleitus is dead,
but his nightingales sing on; and the Spartans at Plataea are not
truly dead since their valour glorifies them and raises them
from Hades. The Greek epitaphs are like the Athenian stelai;
they have the same grace, the same dignified acceptance of the
inevitable, which one sees in those bas-reliefs of the last quiet
farewell. Let us look for a moment at two instances:

Εἶπέ τις, Ἡράκλειτε, τεὸν μόρον, ἐς δέ με δάκρυ
ἤγαγεν, ἐμνήσθην δ' ὁσσάκις ἀμφότεροι
ἥλιον ἐν λέσχῃ κατεδύσαμεν· ἀλλὰ σὺ μέν που,
ξεῖν' Ἁλικαρνησεῦ, τετράπαλαι σποδιή·
αἱ δὲ τεαὶ ζώουσιν ἀηδόνες, ᾗσιν ὁ πάντων
ἁρπακτὴρ Ἀίδης οὐκ ἐπὶ χεῖρα βαλεῖ.[3]

[1] O.B.G.V. 230.   [2] O.B.G.V. 97.   [3] Callimachus, O.B.G.V. 513.

That is well known in William Johnson's translation, as lovely
as it is false in its softness, almost its sentimentality.

'They told me, Heraclitus, they told me you were dead,' etc.
Let me give it you in another rendering, made by a true scholar
whose early death robbed all lovers of Greek of a rare union of
power and sensitiveness, Walter Headlam.

> The brief words, Heraclitus, fell—
> Your death; and with them drew
> Tears to my eyes; old memories thronged—
> How many a time we two
>
> Had sunk the tired-out sun beneath
> Our talk!—Dear friend of old,
> And you there now in Caria—dust,
> A charred ash, ages cold . . . .
>
> But thy sweet voices are not dead,
> Those nightingales yet wake;
> Death with his clutch takes all away,
> But those he shall not take![1]

The whole epitaph is pure Greek; the quiet opening, and then
the shattering news (as quiet as the famous Demosthenic
sentence that describes the time of day and the arrival of the
deadly news[2]); the spirit that will not spare itself the last
refinement of pain nor display it; his friend is τετράπαλαι
σποδιή, and he does not even know where the ashes lie; there are
few monosyllables in poetry that contain such full measure of
controlled anguish as that που (somewhere); but there is no
rebellion, which would be alike useless and undignified; and he
finds what comfort he can, though I think that one feels him
set his teeth again at ἁρπακτήρ. But, moving though this epitaph
is, let us leave the Greek lyric of death with lines even if possible
more purely Greek in their quiet and exquisite grace:

---

[1] *A Book of Greek Verse.*

[2] ἑσπέρα μὲν γὰρ ἦν, ἧκε δ' ἀγγέλλων τις ὡς 'Ελάτεια κατείληπται.
('It was evening, and there came a messenger to report that Elateia
had fallen). *De Corona,* 169.

Ἀστὴρ πρὶν μὲν ἔλαμπες ἐνὶ ζωοῖσιν Ἐῷος·
νῦν δὲ θανὼν λάμπεις Ἕσπερος ἐν φθιμένοις.[1]

And what of the Greek lyric of love? It is a theme handled in
many tempers, lightly, in the dancing measures of those songs of
Anacreon that remind one of the Cavalier lyric in the security
with which they touch the surface without ever breaking it; or
more philosophically, as in one of the greatest of Greek choruses,
that invocation of Sophocles, ἔρως, ἀνίκατε μάχαν.[2] But however the emotion of love is handled, and unfailingly perfect
though the expression of it may be, we become conscious that it
is always the physical passion for beauty that speaks. (It is to the
philosophers that we must turn for a different, and as we should
say higher, conception of the possibilities of love.) But though
this implies a limitation of outlook, it is a limitation and not a
distortion, and within those limits there are many lovely
things. In particular there is one poem that stands in splendid
isolation, perhaps the most poignant love-poem in all secular
literature. If the ideal of poetry is what Milton says it is, to be
simple, sensuous, and passionate, here is a poem which completely realizes it. It is simple both in sentiment and in statement,
but it blazes white-hot with passion. We may leave Greek lyric
with this poem in our ears, the voice of a passion too profound to
lose control of itself.

φαίνεταί μοι κῆνος ἴσος θέοισιν
ἔμμεν᾽ ὤνηρ, ὄττις ἐνάντιός τοι
ἰσδάνει καὶ πλασίον ἆδυ φωνεί-
σας ὑπακούει.[3]

When we turn from Greece to Italy we enter a different
world, and one in which it is at first difficult to find our bearings.

[1] Plato, O.B.G.V. 445 (ii).
  But yesterday you shone among the living,
    The Dawn-star bright;
  Now in the shades you shine, to shadows giving
    The Eve-star's light.
[2] Antigone, 781. 'Love, unconquered in battle.'
[3] Sappho, O.B.G.V. 141.
  Blest beyond earth's bliss, with heaven I deem him
  Blest, the man that in thy presence near thee
  Face to face may sit, and while thou speakest,
    Listening may hear thee.   (Walter Headlam.)

Any one who has at all studied the Roman lyric must have been struck by an odd diversity, even discordance, of impression. The Greek lyrics, however diverse their subjects, are felt to be related to one another, to be the products of the same spirit. But here there seem to be two quite different spirits at work; and so in fact there were. It is worth notice how few of the great Roman poets were Romans born. Virgil and Catullus came from beyond the Po; Horace from south Italy; Seneca and Lucan were Spanish; Terence was an African slave. Almost the only great exception is, as one might expect, Lucretius, who was a Roman aristocrat. And in reading the Roman lyric what we are watching is the spectacle, as has been well said, of a 'great and prosaic people, with a great and prosaic language, directing and controlling to their own ends spiritual forces deeper and more subtle than themselves.'[1] Let us begin our study with the least Roman of Roman poets, who was directed and controlled by nobody, least of all by himself, in whose work you hear the very cry of unsatisfied desire. Catullus abandoned himself with complete surrender to his passion; he is carried hither and thither on the ebb and flow of the tide, and writes not as he would but as he must; and, so writing, he wrote some of the most moving lyrics of the world, whose poignancy is sometimes almost intolerable. It is a commonplace to say that he is neither a Roman nor a Greek, that he had, like Virgil, a large tincture of that 'deep and tender sensibility which is the least Roman thing in the world, and which, in its subtlest manifestations, is perhaps the peculiar possession of the Celt.'[2] Catullus, at least in part, transcends the limitations which seemed to confine the Greek lyric. Whereas we feel that the Greek might have been satisfied with slaking here and now life's daily thirst, we know that in Catullus we have a consuming passion which nothing on this earth can satisfy, but only the everlasting possession of the grave:

[1] H. W. Garrod, preface to *The Oxford Book of Latin Verse*.

[2] *Ibid*. (One can perhaps attempt to approach the 'Celtic spirit,' this 'deep and tender sensibility', more easily by example than by definition. I wonder how many readers will agree with me in finding it exquisitely shown in a poem less well known than I think it deserves, Neil Munro's 'Lament for McLeod of Raasay'?

> A boy, he kept the old tryst of his people
>   With the dark girl Death.)

> soles occidere et redire possunt;
> nobis cum semel occidit brevis lux,
> nox est perpetua una dormienda.[1]

We notice too the instability of the quick shifts of emotion,
passing without warning from vitriolic invective to languor and
yearning. The instance is trite, but so much the most obvious
that it is inevitable:

> cum suis vivat valeatque moechis,
> quos simul complexa tenet trecentos,
> nullum amans vere sed identidem omnium
> ilia rumpens.[2]

There is something of the crazed fury of Othello about it, a
savagery, a hatred of the woman he had loved, a contempt for
his own thraldom, which he will punish by lacerating himself
with the cruellest lash of the imagination, which, like much in
Catullus, resembles but far surpasses the dark bitterness of
Donne. Then, without a break, this:

> nec meum respectet, ut ante, amorem,
> qui illius culpa cecidit velut prati
> ultimi flos, praetereunte postquam
> tactus aratro est.[3]

The storm of fury is over and succeeded by the calm of an
infinite sadness.

But Catullus wrote other things than love-poems, and in them
we are more conscious of direction and control. When he writes

---

[1] 'Suns may sink and arise again to-morrow,
   But when our little light of life is over,
   Rests one unending night for us to sleep through.'
                              (*Carmina*, v; *O.B.L.V.* 86).

[2] 'Let her live happy with her hundred fancies,
   Whom in her arms she holds, one after other,
   Loving not one truly, but of each, unsated,
      Draining the strength out.'
                              (*Carmina*, xi; *O.B.L.V.* 95).

[3] 'Let her not care, as once she did, for my love;
   That by her doing shrivelled lies in death, as
   At the field's edge, touched by the passing ploughshare,
      Lies a dead flower.
                              (*Ibid.*)

of his 'all-but-island, olive-silvery Sirmio' there rings in his voice that deep love of home which is one of the most Roman—and English—things in the world, the spirit that when

> labore fessi venimus larem ad nostrum[1]

can say

> hoc est quod unum est pro laboribus tantis.[2]

Then turn to the poem at his brother's tomb. There is a ring in that poem which you will not match in all the lyrics of the Greeks. Neither Greek nor Roman will lose his dignity in a vain conflict; but whereas the Greek bows his head in acquiescent resignation before the inevitable, the Roman stands up and confronts it. As there is all the Roman pride of empire in the first line, so there is all the grave Roman stoicism in the last.

> multas per gentes et multa per aequora vectus
>   advenio has miseras, frater, ad inferias:
> ut te postremo donarem munere mortis
>   et mutam nequiquam alloquerer cinerem.
> quandoquidem fortuna mihi tete abstulit ipsum,
>   heu miser indigne frater adempte mihi,
> nunc tamen interea haec prisco quae more parentum
>   tradita sunt tristi munere ad inferias,
> accipe fraterno multum manantia fletu,
>   atque in perpetuum, frater, ave atque vale.[3]

I have given that poem in full partly for the pleasure of putting beside it a translation which is a model of what such 'Englishing' can be:

> Over the mighty world's highway,
>   City by city, sea by sea,
> Brother, thy brother comes to pay
>   Pitiful offerings unto thee.
>
> I only ask to grace thy bier
>   With gifts that only give farewell,
> To tell to ears that cannot hear
>   The things that it is vain to tell,

[1] 'Worn with toil we have come home.' (*Carmina*, xxxi; *O.B.L.V.* 82.)   [2] 'This itself is reward enough for all our toil.' (*Ibid.*)
[3] *Carmina*, ci; *O.B.L.V.* 100.

And, idly communing with dust,
  To know thy presence still denied,
And ever mourn forever lost
  A soul that never should have died.

Yet think not wholly vain to-day
  This fashion that our fathers gave
That hither brings me, here to lay
  Some gift of sorrow on thy grave.

Take, brother, gifts a brother's tears
  Bedewed with sorrow as they fell,
And 'Greeting' to the end of years,
  And to the end of years 'Farewell.'[1]

As Catullus turns from Love to Death, he becomes his own master, no longer the Celt but the free Roman. And as we read the Roman lyric we find, I think, that the language and its writers do not easily submit themselves to the tyranny of an emotion so overbearing as passionate love, but that when the subject is death the full power of the great instrument is evoked. It is when the Roman Muse wears the sceptred pall that she moves with the most majestic and stately dignity, *vera incessu patet dea*. To realize the full capacity of the Roman language, the grave utterance of the rulers of the world, read the 'Cornelia' elegy of Propertius: the muffled drums of the greatest of funeral marches can hardly equal the rolling thunder of the opening lines:

Desine, Paulle, meum lacrimis urgere sepulchrum;
  panditur ad nullas ianua nigra preces;
cum semel infernas intrarunt funera leges,
  non exorato stant adamante viae.[2]

Then we go on to read how there is to be silence in Hell as she pleads her case, though 'pleads' is a poor word for a defence which is instinct with the pride of race; and from that she turns

---

[1] H. W. Garrod, in *The Oxford Book of Latin Verse*, p. 460.
[2] 'Give up, Paullus, striving to force my tomb with tears; the black door opens to no prayers of man; when once the bier has entered the jurisdiction of the powers below, the road stands barred by adamant inexorable.' (*Elegiae*, IV. xi; *O.B.L.V.* 179.)

to the home she has left and to her husband, with the very
human doubt as to how blunderingly he will fill her place; and
then she reverts to the hope that she is not unworthy of her
famous line; and as we close the book we are aware that through
the lips of a Roman matron we have heard the voice of
Rome.

But if we wish to hear this voice in all its many accents, grave
and gay, we must turn to the most Roman of the Roman
lyrists. It is useless to try to define the charm of Horace's style;
the attempt has been made again and again, and I suppose that
curiosa felicitas comes nearest to success; but we can at least try
to discover what it is that we find in him that we do not find in
the Greeks. In the first place he is the perfect example of the
polished *urbanitas* of Rome. If not indeed in the earlier Horace of
the Satires and Epodes, at any rate in the later Horace of the
Epistles and the Odes, you find the unerring taste, the perfect
poise, the spirit *dignitatis suae et libertatis alienae memor*, which
mark the gentleman who is also a man of the world. As a result
Horace moves with equal grace from court to country, from
politics to farming, from morality to a dinner invitation. If he
wants to be amusing he moves with complete security on that
tight-rope of serio-comic wit from which so many literary
Blondins have been ignominiously precipitated. For one
example of this wit, consisting in the grave treatment of the
trivial, look at his address to the *triste lignum* that nearly killed
him.[1] And throughout his work we are perpetually happening
on that turn of phrase behind which we catch the twinkle in the
writer's eye. Now this kind of wit is a thing almost unknown in
Greek poetry, though one finds it in the prose writers. Further, as
to Horace's moralizing, it is the stupidest of blunders to suppose
that Horace was a trifler. But whereas Solon and Theognis get
into the pulpit and avowedly preach, Horace explains to you
over a glass of wine by the fire that sound morality is sound
common sense and good citizenship. It is this last phrase that
explains much in Horace, not least the unexpectedly urgent
note that often creeps into his voice.

> virtus, repulsae nescia sordidae,
> intaminatis fulget honoribus,

[1] *Odes*, II. xiii.

> nec sumit aut ponit securis
> arbitrio popularis aurae.[1]

The man who wrote that was no mere man about town. But the
earnestness of which we are so often conscious is never, I think,
what one would call *moral* fervour; it is patriotic. Sir Walter
Raleigh wrote much brilliant literary criticism, and the last
sentences of his *Shakespeare* are well known; but he wrote, I
think, nothing that compares, for quiet power and trenchancy,
with a sentence or two, less well known, in his History of the Air
Force. They illuminate Horace, and are themselves in the best
Roman manner.

> The air service still flourishes; its health depends on a
> secret elixir of immortality, which enables a body to repair
> its severest losses. The name of this elixir is tradition, and
> the greatest of all the achievements of the air service is that
> in a very few years, under the hammer of war, it has
> fashioned and welded its tradition, and has made it sure.
> Critics who speak of what they have not felt and do not
> know have sometimes blamed the air service because, being
> young, it has not the decorum of age. The Latin poet said
> that it is decorous to die for one's country; in that decorum
> the service is perfectly instructed.

That is also Horace's notion of decorum; the decorous,
'the thing to do,' is whatever serves the State; it is the man
who knows *angustam amice pauperiem pati*[2] who makes the
good soldier, the man who is *iustus et propositi tenax*[3] who makes
the good citizen. Therefore, in his quiet but penetrating way, he
teaches his wit-spiced lessons of how to be a good man, because
to be a good man is to be a good Roman. He, like Virgil, in
large measure devoted his art to the service of his country, but

---

[1] *Odes*, III. ii. 17–20.
> True Virtue never knows defeat:
> *Her* robes she keeps unsullied still,
> Nor takes, nor quits, *her* curule seat
> To please a people's veering will.
>   (Conington).

[2] 'to endure the pinch of poverty with good heart' (*Odes*, III. ii. 1).

[3] 'just, and tenacious of what he has determined'—like Wordsworth's Happy Warrior he 'keeps the law in calmness made' (*Odes*,
III. iii, 1).

with very different results, his art being thereby greatly
ennobled and strengthened.

And it is in Horace that you will find that aspect of the
Roman lyric which brings it nearest to our own, the love of
home and the countryside. To the Greeks 'home' in our sense
seems to have meant little. They spent their days in a social
bustle, in agora or pnyx or theatre. The general impression of
their life is of one marked by the lack both of privacy and of the
desire for it. Is there a word in Greek which really translates
'home' or *domus* or *lares et penates*? In Greek lyric any expression
of the joy of return home, or of a quiet hour with a friend, is
uncommon, its rarity emphasized by the delight, but the
surprised delight, with which we chance upon the exceptions.
But the Roman lyric is full of expressions of this feeling;
Catullus' welcome home to Veranius,[1] the poem to Sirmio
already mentioned, Horace's directions to pile the logs high
when the snow is deep on Soracte,[2] the invitation to Maecenas
for the Calends of March.[3] It is the feeling which inspires those
far deeper lines of Lucretius which I quoted earlier:

> Iam iam non domus accipiet te laeta, neque uxor
> Optima, nec dulces occurrent oscula nati
> Praeripere, et tacita pectus dulcedine tangent.[4]

Greece had neither the Roman *domus* nor the Roman *uxor*.

Again, to find the true expression of Roman patriotism, do
not look for it in definite exaltations of Rome and the Roman
empire. You will find them no doubt, and you will find perhaps
the finest example shining out as Roman literature fades into the
twilight, the magnificent tribute paid by a Gaul to the imperial
city that had made the inhabitants of the world her citizens.[5]
But is that the kind of thing that really moved the Roman
heart? Surely not. The true note is in the lines of Horace:

> ille terrarum mihi praeter omnes
> angulus ridet.[6]

[1] *Carmina*, ix; *O.B.L.V.* 79.   [2] *Odes*, I, ix.
[3] *Odes*, III. viii.   [4] p. 9.
[5] Rutilius Claudius Namatianus, *circ.* A.D. 416. 'Urbem fecisti
quod prius orbis erat' ('You have made one city of what was before
a world.') *O.B.L.V.* 373.
[6] *Odes*, II. vi. 13. 'That corner of the world beyond all others is my
delight.'

It matters little where the 'angulus' is; it may be Sirmio, or where the waters flow past fertile Tibur, or a Sabine farm, or the fountain of Bandusia, or Bilbilis; and the poet may be Catullus or Horace or Martial; but the spirit is the same. Home, and the country that he has known and loved from a boy, that is what holds a Roman's devotion. He is a practical person; he loves something territorial and concrete; he prefers a proper name to an abstract noun. It was a sure instinct that made Macaulay write:

> But he saw on Palatinus
> The white porch of his home;
> And he spake to the noble river
> That rolls by the towers of Rome.

Let us make this easy transition to our own English lyric, since nowhere else, perhaps, do we show so clearly our kinship with the great imperial nation of antiquity. We have the same kind of territorial patriotism; we are thoroughly uncomfortable when there is any talk of abstractions; and symbols, except human ones like the royal family, are anathema to us. We can just tolerate John Bull, are a trifle uneasy about the British lion, and frankly derisory about Britannia. If an Englishman says he loves England—in fact wild horses would hardly extract such a phrase from him, but if he were so far to forget himself as to admit that he loved his country—even then it would not be an abstract England that he had in mind; it would not even be that area of ground so many square miles in extent which is coloured red on maps and labelled 'England.' What he would really have at the back of his mind would be that small corner of the world, that *angulus terrarum*, which is dear to him above all others. It may be the Devon combes, or the churches and wind-mills of the fens, or the Cotswold pastures, or Land's End battered by the Atlantic surge; it may be the green swell of the Cheviots, or the bare splendour of great moors, or 'the dark turrets and bastions of the hills of Skye'; or it may be, for that matter, the maelstrom of Piccadilly Circus. But wherever the corner is, it is the pictures of this corner that rise before his eyes, whether he lives in it or has to recall it with a heart-ache from the outposts. Each of us has his own England, or Wales, or Scotland, or Canada, or New Zealand or wherever it is.

> God gave all men all earth to love,
> 　　But since our hearts are small,
> Ordained for each one spot should prove
> 　　Beloved over all.[1]

That is why the most truly imperial of Kipling's poems is one
which has a title more suggestive of Herrick, and is called
'The Flowers.'[2] Here are two stanzas from it:

> Buy my English posies!
> 　　You that scorn the May,
> Won't you greet a friend from home
> 　　Half the world away?
> Green against the draggled drift,
> 　　Faint and frail and first—
> Buy my Northern blood-root
> 　　And I'll know where you were nursed:
> Robin down the logging-road whistles, 'Come to me!'
> Spring has found the maple-grove, the sap is running free;
> All the winds of Canada call the ploughing-rain.
> Take the flower and turn the hour, and kiss your love again!

> Buy my English posies!
> 　　Ye that have your own
> Buy them for a brother's sake
> 　　Overseas, alone.
> Weed ye trample underfoot
> 　　Floods his heart abrim—
> Bird ye never heeded,
> 　　Oh, she calls his dead to him!
> Far and far our homes are set round the Seven Seas;
> Woe for us if we forget, we who hold by these!
> Unto each his mother-beach, bloom and bird and land—
> Masters of the Seven Seas, oh, love and understand!

This deep love of the country is one of the most pervading
inspirations of English lyric. It may be a love of nature not
specifically localized, as in 'Sumer is icumen in,' or Shakespeare's daisies pied and violets blue, or Marvell annihilating
all that's made to a green thought in a green shade, or Milton's

---

[1] Kipling, *Sussex* in *The Five Nations*.　　　　[2] in *The Seven Seas*.

shepherd telling his tale under the hawthorn, or Gray's lowing herd on the lea, or Flecker's cry

Oh shall I never never be home again?
Meadows of England, shining in the rain,
Spread wide your daisied lawns . . .

Or it may be, characteristically, more particular, Kirconnell Lea, or Leven Water, or that huddle of half comic, half heart-twisting, names in 'the comely land of Teme, and Lugg, and Clent, and Clee, and Wyre,'[1] or Bredon Hill, or the Old Vicarage at Grantchester.

But it is there always, and it comes through most piercingly in the exiles' songs—Stevenson in the South Seas writing to Crockett:

Blows the wind to-day, and the sun and the rain are flying,
Blows the wind on the moors to-day and now,
Where about the graves of the martyrs the whaups are crying,
My heart remembers how!

or the great admiral, low on the field of his fame:

Only to look once more on the land of the memories of child-
hood,
Forgetting weary winds and barren foam:
Only to bid farewell to the combe and the orchard and the
moorland,
And sleep at last among the fields of home![2]

or the Jacobite exile longing for

The lordly strand of Northumberland,
And the goodly towers thereby;[3]

or the other Jacobite who

Heard on Lavernia Scargill's whispering trees,
And pined by Arno for his lovelier Tees.[4]

Through all these exiles' songs thrills that passionate love of their own country which for the men and women of our race is their true patriotism, which they feel in the deep heart's core,

[1] Masefield, *London Town*.
[2] H. Newbolt, *The Death of Admiral Blake*.
[3] Swinburne, *A Jacobite's Exile*.
[4] Macaulay, *A Jacobite's Epitaph*.

but which only their poets can make articulate for them. And
it is this passion that informs that loveliest of all wanderers'
laments,

> From the lone shieling of the misty island
> Mountains divide us, and the waste of seas,
> But still the blood is strong, the heart is Highland,
> And we in dreams behold the Hebrides.[1]

And underlying much of this feeling for the country, and
sometimes expressed, is an element in our national character
which does nothing to diminish the bewilderment with which
the foreigner regards that complex compound. For all our love
of the concrete and dislike of the abstract, we have an odd
tolerance for 'faerie'—indeed much more than mere tolerance.
It has to be a particular *kind* of faerie, not the tinselled airy-
fairy kind, but well down to earth, the kind represented by
Puck (whether Shakespeare's or Kipling's) who is as 'mere
English' as Gloriana herself. But when it is of that kind we
respond to it eagerly, so that a phrase like 'till the sure magic
strike' really means something to us, especially when the magic
is *of* the earth, of the land which can exert its potent witcheries
over 'returning strangers.' 'Over their heads' (the speaker is
'the land of their fathers')

> Over their heads in the branches
> Of their new-bought, ancient trees,
> I weave an incantation
> And draw them to my knees.[2]

But you will notice that the accompaniments of the incantation
are as concrete as ever they can be, 'Scent of smoke in the
evening, Smell of rain in the night.' This power of reacting to
the magic of earth lies, I think, deep at the heart of an Englishman's love of his own land.

> She is not any common Earth,
> Water or wood or air,
> But Merlin's Isle of Gramarye,
> Where you and I will fare![3]

---

[1] 'Canadian Boat Song' (authorship uncertain.)
[2] Kipling, *The Recall* (after 'An Habitation Enforced' in *Actions and
Reactions*).   [3] Kipling, *Puck's Song* (in *Puck of Pook's Hill*).

What of other aspects of the English lyric? Let us descend for
the moment from the heights of patriotism, however expressed,
to more trival subjects; drinking songs for example. We looked
rather cursorily at the kind of thing which a Greek sang when
he was revelling: I say revelling rather than drinking since the
latter suggests a certain repose which is absent from the σκόλια.
They are light, dancing, excited. You feel that they are the
songs of light-headed excitable persons to whom wine is a not
very important adjunct to a revel. There is nothing at all to
show that the Greeks had any proper, solid, and discerning
appreciation of good wine. The Romans knew better than this,
and had some notion of circumstantial detail. Horace would
seldom be so crude as to say merely φέρ' οἶνον (bring wine).
That is the vulgar attitude of the man who merely wants to get
drunk. Horace has the loving particularity of the connoisseur;
his wine is a Sabine vintage four years in wood; or a nine-year-
old cask of Alban; or he warns his guest that he must be content
with Caecuban, not Falernian, but he has some good Caecuban,
well cobwebbed from his grandfather's cellar; or for yet
another occasion the wine must be 'languidior'.[1] For the
purposes of the English lyric it is unfortunate that the national
drink should have little diversity, nor any proper names valuable
for literary decoration. It cannot be pretended that either 'beer'
or 'ale' is particularly euphonious, or indeed has any merit except
a monosyllabic and uncompromisingly British air. However, let
us see what the English writer makes of this material. It may
be the not unaptly named Prelate of Bath and Wells, Bishop
John Still (if it was he who wrote the song), who

> stuffed his skin so full within
> Of jolly good ale and old;[2]

or it may be that admirable anonymous writer who wrote two
songs to tobacco and ale, the second of which opens thus:

> When as the chill Charokko blows,
>   And Winter tells a heavy tale;
> When pyes and daws and rooks and crows
> Sit cursing of the frosts and snows;
>   Then give me ale.[3]

---

[1] *Odes*, I. ix. 7; IV. xi. 1, 2; I. xx. 9–11 and xxxvii. 5, 6; III. xxi. 8.
[2] From *Gammer Gurton's Needle*.   [3] *O.B.E.V.* 390, II.

These have none of Horace's perfect artistry, but there is a fine solid gusto about them both, a deliberate smack of the lips, that is typically English; and even when the lyric becomes more definitely a drinking catch, like the σκόλια, there is still a power about it, a roll of bass voices, which is absent from the lighter music of the Greeks. Take for illustration Peacock's *Three Men of Gotham*, or still better that uproariously sweeping chorus in which you can hear the pounding on the table in Headlong Hall:

> A heeltap! a heeltap! I never could bear it!
> So fill me a bumper, a bumper of claret!
> Let the bottle pass freely, don't shirk it nor spare it,
> For a heeltap! a heeltap! I never could bear it!

If we want to find the perfection of light dancing wit we shall find it brought to a trimmer exquisiteness by the Cavalier lyrists and by Prior than by any classical writer. Horace can do it, but it is only by taking thought that he adds this particular grace to his many others; whereas the English poets, however much of the *summa ars* they are in fact using, appear at any rate to do it without a thought, with as wellbred an ease as they dusted the snuff from their lace ruffles. Take Suckling's famous lines that begin with solicitude over the lover's complexion and end with so airy a dismissal; or his cry:

> Out upon it, I have loved
> Three whole days together!

and the exquisitely trivial meteorological proviso of the next two lines; or Prior's lines put into the mouth of a lady dedicating her mirror to Venus;[1] or those others which have all the classic balance and a more than classic grace:

> For, as our different ages move,
>   'Tis so ordain'd (would Fate but mend it!),
> That I shall be past making love
>   When she begins to comprehend it.[2]

Now Martial has a great reputation for finished and polished wit; but even his more readable efforts at their most finished are clumsy, heavy, and laboured beside the butterfly lightness of

---

[1] *O.B.E.V.* 426.   [2] *Ibid.* 423.

the English work, and the Greek lyric in its extant examples hardly attempts this vein.

To return from these trivialities, delicate and delightful though they are, to one of the great lyric subjects. What of the English love lyric? What can we find out from it about the English? If we compare it with the Greek and Roman lyric we are at once conscious of a wide difference that has its roots much deeper than in differences of language or even of temperament. The truth is that the whole conception of love in England, at least from the days of chivalry onwards, is something so entirely different from that of classical Greece and Rome that a comparison is none too easy. We are in a world where the whole position of women is different. When you find a man of Plato's stamp, of superlative intellectual power, deep humanity and lofty idealism, in his ideal state raising women, as 'guardians,' to an equality with men, but relegating them, as women, to the position of breeding machines, you know exactly where you are. Matters were better in the Rome of the Republic and of Augustus; we have the lovely lyric of Acme and Septimius,[1] and some moving expressions of married love; but much worse under the later Empire. And I do not think it is going too far to say that the phrase the 'marriage of true minds' would to a Greek or Roman have been meaningless. Here are the first eight lines of a sonnet by Sidney, and a lyric by Robert Bridges.

> My true love hath my heart, and I have his,
>   By just exchange one for another given:
> I hold his dear, and mine he cannot miss,
>   There never was a better bargain driven:
> His heart in me keeps him and me in one,
>   My heart in him his thoughts and senses guides:
> He loves my heart for once it was his own,
>   I cherish his because in me it bides:[2]

> Since thou, O fondest and truest,
> Hast loved me best and longest,
> And now with trust the strongest
> The joy of my heart renewest;

[1] Catullus, xlv (*O.B.L.V.* 83).
[2] Sidney, from *Arcadia* (*O.B.E.V.* 88).

Since thou art dearer and dearer
While other hearts grow colder
And ever, as love is older,
More lovingly drawest nearer:

Since now I see in the measure
Of all my giving and taking,
Thou wert my hand in the making,
The sense and soul of my pleasure;

The good I have ne'er repaid thee
In heaven I pray be recorded,
And all thy love rewarded
By God, thy master that made thee.[1]

They are separated in time by three hundred years, in feeling by no distinguishable interval. They are songs of spiritual love, and they and others like them are perhaps the peculiar glory of the English lyric. I do not mean that this is the only or even the chief type of English love lyric. We find the sheer love of physical beauty which appears in its artificial form in the inventories of the lady's charms with conventional comparisons, or Shakespeare's counterblast to that; and in its more frankly sensuous form in Donne or in *The Eve of St. Agnes*; and we find the most delicate filigree work in the same vein, 'Whenas in silks my Julia goes.' There is the pain of love, sinking sometimes to a deeper note, as in Campion's great lyric 'When thou must home to shades of underground,' with its sombre bitterness and tremendous climax; or expressed with passionate anger and revolt in Donne. But even in Donne there appears also the spiritual and intellectual aspect:

Our souls, (which to advance their state,
Were gone out,) hung 'twixt her, and me.[2]

I suggest that in the English love lyric, as elsewhere in English poetry, we find two distinct ways of regarding love, not antagonistic but complementary, one the purely sensuous and physical, which may lead to exquisite lyric or to the frank coarseness of the Elizabethans, and the other a conception of a

---

[1] Bridges, *Shorter Poems*, III, 17.   [2] *The Extasie* (*O.B.E.V.* 198).

spiritual relation which raises and transmutes the physical
passion into something finer; there is, I think, yet a third way,
but it is one which has not often been presented in our lyric,
perhaps for the very reason which makes it the most satisfying.
In this the relation of the lovers is taken to be one in which
spiritual harmony and physical passion co-exist, with no
question of either dominating over or transmuting the other,
but combining in equi-valence to create a unified and transcendent experience. But that presentation can be made only by
a man who has not only strong emotions but also a cool intellectual grasp of the difficult duality of human nature. And
such a tempered balance seems to be seldom the kindler of lyric
inspiration.

We find those three ways, but I suggest that what we never
find, what indeed would seem to an Englishman a sort of
confusion of thought, is the idea of physical passion raised to a
pitch of intensity at which in its own right it becomes spiritual.
Is that, I wonder, why Rossetti's *House of Life*, wonderful
sequence though it is, makes many English readers slightly
uncomfortable, aware of something exotic about it. As examples
of our three 'English' ways there are Meredith's *Love in the
Valley*, Browning's *By the Fireside*, and the first four poems in
Meredith's *A Reading of Life* together with *The Extasie* taken as
a whole.

Before we move on to consider how the English lyrists have
handled the other of the two great lyric subjects, we may
perhaps pause for a moment to wander a few yards down one
or two byways. Any one, I think, who compares the lyrical
poetry of the three languages must be struck by the impression
of much richer variety which the English lyric produces. This
variety is due at least in part to the fact that the English
lyrists found subjects either demanding, or at least permit-
ting, lyric treatment, subjects which exerted no such demand
or extended no such permission to their forerunners. Here,
for example, is an epitaph written by a man who died in
1523.

> O mortal folk, you may behold and see
>   How I lie here, sometime a mighty knight:
> The end of joy and all prosperitee
>   Is death at last, thorough his course and might:

> After the day there cometh the dark night,
>   For though the day be never so long,
>   At last the bells ringeth to evensong. [1]

Now what is it in that comparatively common-place poem that strikes with so arresting an impact on the mind attuned to the classic lyric? Surely the bells, and all that they conjure up in the imagination, 'the sound of church bells, that peculiar creation of mediaeval age, which falls upon the ear like the echo of a vanished world'. [2] Vanished perhaps for us; but for Horace and Sappho it had never been born.

The religious motive is indeed pervasive in English lyric, whether it has to do with the religious conception of immortality, or with the figures of religion, or with the religious impulse in general. We find Chaucer, who cannot be called a profoundly serious poet, becoming unexpectedly moved, and therefore deeply moving, as in the ABC or the account of the small boy's cry of 'Alma Redemptoris Mater'; and we jump five hundred years to find Flecker, from whose poems one would be hard put to it to extract anything specifically religious, yet writing one of his most exquisite lyrics on the Magi, in which the effect depends not indeed on an acceptance, but on an appreciation, of a religious significance. Then there is all the poetry which is inspired by religious symbolism, especially by the book of Revelation and the hope of immortality, like

> Hierusalem, my happy home,
>   When shall I come to thee?
> When shall my sorrows have an end,
>   Thy joys when shall I see?
>
> Thy walls are made of precious stones,
>   Thy bulwarks diamonds square;
> Thy gates are of right orient pearl,
>   Exceeding rich and rare.
>
> Quite through the streets, with silver sound,
>   The flood of Life doth flow;
> Upon whose banks on every side
>   The wood of Life doth grow.

---

[1] Stephen Hawes (*O.B.E.V.* 33).
[2] Froude, *History of England*, c. I.

> Our Lady sings *Magnificat*
>   With tones surpassing sweet;
> And all the virgins bear their part,
>   Sitting about her feet.
>
> Hierusalem, my happy home,
>   Would God I were in thee!
> Would God my woes were at an end,
>   Thy joys that I might see![1]

or, at a higher level of poetical accomplishment, this of
Vaughan, at his most direct and loveliest,

> My soul, there is a country
>   Far beyond the stars,
> Where stands a wingèd sentry
>   All skilful in the wars:
> There, above noise and danger,
>   Sweet peace sits crown'd with smiles,
> And One born in a manger
>   Commands the beauteous files.
> He is thy gracious friend,
>   And—O my soul, awake!—
> Did in pure love descend
>   To die here for thy sake.
> If thou canst get but thither,
>   There grows the flower of Peace,
> The Rose that cannot wither,
>   Thy fortress, and thy ease.
> Leave then thy foolish ranges;
>   For none can thee secure
> But One who never changes—
>   Thy God, thy life, thy cure.[2]

There is Sir Walter Raleigh with his scallop shell of quiet; there
is, three centuries later, perhaps the most secure and satisfying
of our religious poets, Christina Rossetti. And finally there is
all the poetry of the great mystics, Crawshaw flaming and
ardent, Vaughan illumined by the light that he so loved,
Francis Thompson with his almost hectic splendour of diction,

---

[1] Anon. (*O.B.E.V.* 61).
[2] *Silex Scintillans*, 'Peace' (*O.B.E.V.* 363).

Herbert of all English poets the most beautifully at ease in Sion. Whether one rates mystical poetry high or low depends no doubt on temperament, but at least the mystical poets extended the range of the lyric by using it to express a type of emotional experience which, whether or not it had existed before, had not commonly used poetry as its channel. In the classical lyric there are magnificent invocations to the members of the Olympian hierarchy, but hardly a trace of that mystic element without which religion is little more than picturesque mythology.

If religion is a new subject, even newer is science. It is true that classical writers wrote about scientific subjects in verse, and even sometimes in poetry; but they were very far from writing lyric poetry about them. Science lived in a speculative realm of its own, apart from the ordinary life of men which is the realm of lyric. But as soon as science, particularly in its guise of 'applied' science, breaks the barriers and becomes part and parcel of life, then its products and its tools become something which the lyric poets can without incongruity handle. If we follow the line of our lyric poetry down from Donne constructing his famous simile of the compasses, through Wordsworth and a good deal of Tennyson, to Brooke writing of the 'keen Unpassioned beauty of a great machine,' and Day Lewis of 'twin poles energic that generate a spark,' we shall find the footprints of science more and more deeply marked.

But the rich variety of English lyric is not the outcome only of new subjects. It is the outcome also of a wide diversity of temper in handling the old subjects. We have Coleridge and Keats distilling for us the essence of the 'romantic,' the form elaborate, the outlines sometimes deliberately a little blurred, the compelling mystery of Gothic architecture in the moonlight; but we have also Landor and Housman to show that we can rival the classic writers in their own field, deep emotion ridden on the curb, strong simplicity of form and clean-cut clarity of outline; and for that matter we have de la Mare using the methods of the classic writers to transport us with a wizard's easy mastery to the fairy lands of the romantic. We have *Kubla Khan*, and the *Epitaph on an Army of Mercenaries*, and *The Listeners*.

This diversity of temper is seen in the different ways in which the subject of Death is treated; and with one or two illustrations of them this cursory examination may conclude.

Death be not proud, though some have called thee
Mighty and dreadful, for thou art not so,
For those, whom thou think'st thou dost overthrow,
Die not, poor death, nor yet canst thou kill me.
From rest and sleep, which but thy pictures be,
Much pleasure, then from thee much more must flow,
And soonest our best men with thee do go,
Rest of their bones, and souls' delivery.
Thou art slave to Fate, Chance, kings, and desperate men,
And dost with poison, war, and sickness dwell,
And poppy, or charms can make us sleep as well,
And better than thy stroke; why swell'st thou then?
One short sleep past, we wake eternally,
And death shall be no more; death, thou shalt die.[1]

A late lark twitters from the quiet skies:
And from the west,
Where the sun, his day's work ended,
Lingers as in content,
There falls on the old, gray city
An influence luminous and serene,
A shining peace.

The smoke ascends
In a rosy-and-golden haze. The spires
Shine and are changed. In the valley
Shadows rise. The lark sings on. The sun,
Closing his benediction,
Sinks, and the darkening air
Thrills with a sense of the triumphing night—
Night with her train of stars
And her great gift of sleep.

So be my passing!
My task accomplish'd and the long day done,
My wages taken, and in my heart

[1] Donne, *Holy Sonnets*, **xx** (*O.B.E.V.* 202).

> Some late lark singing,
> Let me be gather'd to the quiet west,
> The sundown splendid and serene,
> Death.[1]

And lastly, three stanzas of a poem which has the dignity of the Cornelia elegy, the restraint of Callimachus' lament, the secure control of either as it rises to its climax; it is also as English as anything can be. Here are the first and the two last stanzas of *Elegy on a Lady whom Grief for the Death of her Betrothed Killed*:[2]

> Assemble, all ye maidens, at the door,
> And all ye loves, assemble; far and wide
> Proclaim the bridal, that proclaimed before
> Has been deferred to this late eventide:
> > For on this night the bride,
> > The days of her betrothal over,
> > Leaves the parental hearth for evermore;
> To-night the bride goes forth to meet her lover.
>
> .   .   .   .
>
> Now to the river bank the priests are come;
> The bark is ready to receive its freight;
> Let some prepare her place therein, and some
> Embark the litter with its slender weight:
> > The rest stand by in state
> > And sing her a safe passage over;
> > While she is oared across to her new home,
> Into the arms of her expectant lover.
>
> And thou, O lover, that art on the watch,
> Where, on the banks of the forgetful streams,
> The pale indifferent ghosts wander, and snatch
> The sweeter moments of their broken dreams,—
> > Thou, when the torchlight gleams,
> > When thou shalt see the slow procession,
> > And when thine ears the fitful music catch,
> Rejoice, for thou art near to thy possession.

[1] Henley, *Echoes*, xxxv (*O.B.E.V.* 843)
[2] Bridges, *Shorter Poems*, I. 14.

CHAPTER FIVE

DRAMA

WE COME NOW TO THE LAST OF OUR LITERARY FORMS, DRAMA. Of so wide a field it is clear that we can do no more than make a preliminary triangulation, in the course of which you may find tracts of which you will wish to conduct for yourselves a more deliberate survey. In a single chapter I can do little more than point out some significant peculiarities of Greek drama, particularly in the circumstances of its presentation, and suggest certain resemblances and contrasts between it and our own drama, particularly the Elizabethan. Of the *influence* of Greek or of Senecan drama I propose to say as little as possible.

First, as to the circumstances of the presentation of Greek tragedy. All the conflicting theories as to its origin agree at least in this, that it arose from some form of religious observance, involving choric dance and song. Therefore—religious tradition being more tenacious of life than any other form of tradition— the chorus was always an integral part of Greek tragedy, and in its earlier examples of greater importance than the individual actors. The main part, therefore, of a Greek theatre was not at first a stage, but an 'orchestra,' a circular dancing floor. At the back of this by degrees there came to be a stage. At the back of the stage was first a σκηνή, a tent or booth acting as a green room, and forming also a rough background: this developed later into a more permanent and elaborate background of a palace front with central doors. The seats were arranged tier above tier round about five-eighths of the orchestra, and they accommodated many thousands of spectators. The theatre was open to the sky. The actors wore masks. There were never more than three speaking parts on the stage at any one time: and the chorus after their first entrance remained in the orchestra until their final exit closed the play.

Now you will recognize that these circumstances make the representation of a Greek tragedy something quite different from any dramatic entertainment of which we have experience. The majority of the audience was sitting at a very considerable distance from the actors. (If you will imagine one end of an 'Olympics' Stadium being used as an auditorium, with the orchestra and stage at the centre of the diameter of the semi-circle,[1] you will have a reasonably clear picture of the situation.) In consequence, no subtleties of facial expression could in any event be effective, whether the actors wore masks or not. Further, any slight gesticulation would be lost: (i.e. the drama as a spectacle was at exactly the opposite pole from a close-up on a film). What the audience watched was something more like a distant group of coloured and moving statuary than a group of actors in our sense: *coloured* statuary, since the sweeping robes which the actors wore were brilliantly coloured. The result was that the dramatist had to rely for his effects almost entirely upon the mere word. And scenery was of the simplest, as indeed in an open air theatre it must be. In a curious way the wheel of dramatic technique came full circle with the introduction of radio, and anyone who today listens to a sound-broadcast play is listening to a performance which depends not mainly, but entirely, upon the mere word, the expressiveness of the human voice, and the vividness of his own imagination, with no adventitious aids to lean upon. And, if one's imagination is alive, such a play, if it is suitable for such presentation, can be startingly effective. The limitation in Greek tragedy of the number of characters on the stage at one time made for simplicity of effect: it almost forebade complexity of plot, and forced the dramatist to concentrate upon the slow increase of tension in working out a simple plot, since in a complicated plot the different threads must, at some point or other, be represented on the stage by different speaking characters. And

[1] Or, let us say, half of the Yale Bowl, or any other great amphi-theatre.

attention was still further concentrated upon the actual words
of the drama by the fact that the story in its main outlines was
almost always known to the audience, since it was drawn either
from history or, much more frequently, from familiar myth.
What the characters *did*, therefore, was known and unalterable:
all that fell within the dramatist's scope for displaying his own
particular dramatic skill was what the characters *felt*, the words
in which they expressed their feelings, and certain minor modi-
fications in the detail of the plot. Within these limits there was
of course considerable latitude, as one can see by a comparison of
the figures of Electra and Orestes as drawn by the three great
tragedians; but it was a latitude in psychology and poetry
rather than in dramatic structure. Finally, and most important,
there was the inevitable chorus. In early Greek tragedy it was a
leading actor, as in the *Suppliants* of Aeschylus, where it is the
fate of the chorus which is at stake. Later it became a group of
people interested in the action, and making relevant comments
on it, and then gradually it sank more and more to the position
of incidental music; but it was always there, and its effect on
Greek tragedy was profound. One hears a great deal of 'the
unities,' which Aristotle is supposed to have laid down as rules
to which tragedy must conform. As a matter of fact, Aristotle is
concerned to examine the actual practice of the tragedians
rather than to lay down rules. And even in examining practice
he does not mention the unity of place at all, the nearest he
gets to the unity of action is to say that an episodic plot is a bad
one, and his only allusion to the unity of time is to say that the
action of a play is usually contained within one circuit of the
sun. But it is true that in practice the tragedians did, as a rule,
conform to the unities: and I think one can fairly say that,
though the unities give a certain completeness and finish which
were in accordance with Greek artistic ideals, the unities, or
certainly two of them, were forced upon the dramatist by the
presence of the chorus, so long, that is, as any verisimilitude was
to be maintained. Here were twelve or fifteen (the number
varied) old men of Argos or young women of somewhere else,
assembled in front of the palace of their own town. How was any
dramatist to account reasonably for their presence in the next
scene in front of the palace in some quite different town, even
supposing they were to leave the orchestra, which in fact they

did not? And until the chorus had degenerated into mere musical interlude, it was equally difficult to manage any considerable interval of time, and things were made easier if the imagined time of action was approximately coterminous with the time of representation, or at least did not exceed 'one circuit of the sun.' It is noteworthy that of the only two instances in extant Greek drama where the unity of place is broken, one is slight and easily accounted for—the sailors of Ajax appearing first in front of his quarters and then some short way off on the beach, seeking his body; and the other is the exception which illustrates the rule—the Furies in the *Eumenides* have supernatural means of transport, and it is both natural and possible for them to pursue Orestes from Delphi to Athens.

Here then are the conditions under which Greek tragedy was produced. When in connection with them you consider the Greek artistic instinct, the love of restraint, the love of balance, of finish, coherence, symmetry, and the keen intellect, you are not surprised that Greek tragedy was what it was. To try to get some kind of impression of a performance in a Greek theatre, and of a typical Greek tragedy, will you imagine yourselves watching in the theatre at Athens two great dramas: the first, on a historical theme, belongs to a comparatively early stage of development; the other is by common consent the most finished extant masterpiece of the Greek stage.

Imagine yourself then on a spring day in 472 B.C., one of an audience of some 15,000 in the great theatre of Dionysus on the south-eastern slopes of the Acropolis. In front and below you is an open space in which the chorus move and sing: beyond this is a structure like a palace front. It has just represented the palace of Phineus and is going to represent the palace in Susa. You are sitting on hard wooden boards, and though you have a cushion it does not seem either so thick or so soft as it did at the beginning of the day. The theatre is open to the sky, and the sun is every moment getting hotter. You are uncomfortably crowded, and your left-hand neighbour is a man whose bad manners the comic writers have often pilloried—deservedly pilloried, you are beginning to think. Altogether, life in a democratic city seems to you less pleasant in practice than in theory. But your right-hand neighbour is a man who fought beside you at Salamis eight years ago, and you are both eagerly expectant of

the play just going to begin. You know your poet well, and are
confident that he will not disappoint you: he has a great
subject and will deal with it in the grand style; besides, he
knows what he is talking about. He fought at Marathon and
Salamis himself, and you suspect—what his own epitaph on
himself will later show[1]—that he is prouder of that fact than of
all his dramatic triumphs.

And now the heralds come in, commanding silence; and as a
hush falls over the theatre the chorus enter, a small group of
old men, marching to the time of their own chanting. They are
foreigners by their dress, Persians as the third word of their
chant makes certain; and in a moment you are far away from
Athens, and stand before the palace in Susa, watching. They
tell you that they alone were left behind when the great host
went out to conquer Greece; they give name after name of
the captains who have gone to war and the far-stretching lands
that they came from; and as their voices thrill with the pride of
empire your own heart feels an answering thrill of pride, mixed
with a certain awe, to think that it was this unnumbered
multitude you helped to conquer. But the old men are not quite
easy at heart. No news has come: can the gods have destroyed
the host? Enter Atossa, queen of Persia, widow of Darius,
mother of Xerxes. She is splendidly adorned with barbaric
pearl and gold, and rides in a chariot. Her heart, too, is
troubled, and she relates a dream which seems to her ominous.
The elders advise sacrifice to the gods and especial prayer to
Darius. She asks for information as to Hellas, and the elders
give it her. Enter a messenger: he gives news of the complete
overthrow of the Persian host. The elders break out into wild
lamentation. Atossa, at first overwhelmed, has now rallied and
is the queen again. She asks for more details. The messenger
gives first the news that Xerxes is alive, and then a list of the
dead; and in the welter of strange barbaric names your ear
catches half a dozen that you heard in the first triumphant
chorus. And then, in answer to a question from Atossa, the
messenger launches out into the tale of Salamis; and before six
lines have been spoken the theatre is as hushed as a theatre of
the dead, and you know that you are listening to a tale of
battle told as no such tale has ever been told yet, nor perhaps

[1] *O.B.G.V.* 269.

ever will be in the world again. The last eight years of your life
vanish like a dream, as they do for many in the theatre at that
moment. You stand again on your ship's deck, watching the
lines of Persian ships grow clearer in the grey dawn; you hear
again the paean that rose as the level sunlight touched the waves;
you feel again the shock as your ship's ram drives home in a
Persian's side; and you stand again at the day's end looking
over a sea covered with wreckage and the corpses of the dead.
When you come to yourself again, Atossa has gone out and the
old men are chanting a lament. Atossa re-enters, this time on
foot and as a suppliant, and at her command the old men sing
an outlandish incantation to Darius. As it ends the ghost of
Darius rises and, in the dialogue which follows, makes plain,
what has been often hinted already, that this disaster is the
doom of the gods upon arrogance. The phantom descends,
Atossa goes into the palace, and the doors have hardly closed
behind her when Xerxes enters. With a long passage of wailing
and lamentations between him and the chorus, always barbaric
and sometimes ridiculous, the play closes, and he and they go
out. You come back from the palace in Susa to the theatre of
Dionysus in Athens. You slowly wake to the discomfort of your
surroundings: the seat is harder, the sun hotter, than they were
an hour ago. But you have had an unforgettable experience:
you have seen the *Persians* of Aeschylus.

As you think the play over at home in the evening, you are at
first a little disappointed. Why was there no eulogy of Athens?
Why no mention from beginning to end of any individual
Greek? Has not Aeschylus missed a great chance? Yes: he has,
deliberately, missed the chance of an easy triumph; but he has
achieved a hard one. Anyone can make obvious appeals to
popular patriotic sentiment: there is no appeal so immediate
or so transient. Athens could have been extolled as the saviour
of Greece, which indeed she was. But this is only part of the
truth. The whole truth, as Aeschylus sees it, is this, that the
battle of Salamis is something much greater, much grander,
than a historical episode, than the triumph of a single city, or even
of all Greece, over a barbarian country; it is the triumph of right
over wrong, of the justice of God over the presumption of men.
He sees it, to use the stock phrase, *sub specie aeternitatis*, an
incident in an age-long conflict: and as he sees it, so he draws it.

Consequently the *Persae* is marked not merely by masterful artistic technique, but by a sweep and grandeur of moral outlook.

Now for our second instance. The time is some forty years later. During those years Sophocles has risen to prominence and has even on occasion defeated Aeschylus. Today he is competing with the *Oedipus Tyrannus*. You know the main outlines of the story perfectly well, how Laius and Jocasta, fearing the fulfil-ment of the prophecy that their son should slay his father and marry his mother, exposed the child Oedipus on Mount Cithaeron, how he was rescued and brought up abroad, how later, journeying to Thebes, he met Laius and killed him, arrived at Thebes, solved the riddle of the Sphinx, married Jocasta and reigned as king; how the truth was exposed, Jocasta killed herself, and Oedipus put out his own eyes. Your interest, then, is concentrated upon watching how Sophocles will handle the well-known story. You know at least that there will be no cheap appeals to sentiment.

The scene of the play is in front of the palace of Oedipus in Thebes. Before the great doors there is an altar, and two more altars at the sides. Suppliants are seated on the steps. The Priest of Zeus is standing facing the central doors. These are thrown open and Oedipus, the king, enters. He asks what their request is. The priest explains that in the distress of the city, stricken by plague, they turn to Oedipus, who before delivered them from the Sphinx. Oedipus replies that he has already sent Creon, his brother-in-law, to Delphi to inquire of Apollo's oracle what can be done to stay the plague. At this moment Creon enters. He explains that Phoebus has directed them to cleanse the city by banishing or killing the man who killed Laius, Oedipus' predecessor on the throne. Oedipus then asks how Laius met his end. He was on his way to Delphi, says Creon, and the only survivor of his company was a man who fled, and said that they had been attacked by a company of robbers. Creon explains further, in answer to Oedipus' somewhat indignant question, that there had been no further inquiry because their attention had been distracted by the more immediate trouble with the Sphinx. Oedipus announces that he will start the inquiry from the beginning. You will observe already the skill of the thing. Here is the great king trusted by his people; yet the spectators know that the blood-guilt is on him, and they watch him making, quite unconsciously, the first step along the road to revelation. If the survivor's account had been of a solitary wayfarer Oedipus' suspicions might have been already aroused. But as it is, he has no thought but to save his city by carrying out the god's command. Oedipus and Creon go into the palace and the suppliants depart. Into the empty orchestra enter the chorus of Theban elders, describing the plague, and praying for succour to Apollo, Athene, and Artemis.

Oedipus re-enters; he explains that, as he was not in the the country when Laius was killed, he needs help in his search. He announces free pardon to anyone who will reveal the slayer of Laius. He excommunicates the slayer, invokes a solemn curse upon him, and, as if this was not irony enough, he goes on to pray that if the slayer has become an inmate of his own house he himself may suffer the same curse. Oedipus is the man to conduct the inquiry since he has inherited Laius' throne, and— here the second thread of the plot is introduced—his wife. And there is a horrible irony in the Greek, not reproducible in translation, which hints at Oedipus' relation to Jocasta. The chorus suggest taking counsel of the seer Teiresias; this, says Oedipus, has already been suggested by Creon, and Teiresias has been summoned; the chorus go on to say that the rumour was that wayfarers had killed Laius. This is nearer the truth, but is assumed by Oedipus to be merely a variant on robbers. It is still the plural. But we feel that Oedipus is standing upon the edge of revelation into which the most casual word may precipitate him. Enter Teiresias. At first he refuses to speak— because he knows the truth; then, as Oedipus' natural anger rises at the man who knows the truth which will save the city, and yet will not reveal it, he speaks. 'I say that thou art the slayer of the man whose slayer thou seekest': and 'I say that thou hast been living in unguessed shame with thy nearest kin.' Oedipus, who at the best of times is hot-tempered, is now nearly beside himself with rage, regards Teiresias' words as insults, and does not pause for an instant to consider whether they may be true. Rather he suspects nothing but a design of Creon to usurp the throne, using Teiresias as his tool. He sneers at Teiresias and oracles in general, contrasting his own skill in the matter of the Sphinx's riddle. Teiresias makes a dignified

but ominous reply, which still further inflames Oedipus, who
drives Teiresias away. The latter in his final speech makes his
meaning more explicit. 'I will go when I have said what I came
to say, with no fear of your frown. You have no power to harm
me. I tell you this. The man for whom you are making tedious
search, with your threats and your proclamations about the
death of Laius, that man is here. He passes as a foreigner who
has come to live among us, but soon he will be shown to be a
Theban born; and small joy will he have of his fortune. The
see-er shall be blind and the wealthy man a beggar; and he shall
fare out to a foreign land, feeling the way before him with his
staff. He shall be shown at once brother and father of his own
children, son and husband of the woman who bore him, slayer
of the father with whose seed he has mingled his own. Go in, and
think upon these things.' Oedipus withdraws into the palace,
and the chorus declares that they cannot understand this
strange charge against Oedipus, and will not believe without
proof. Creon enters, indignant at Oedipus' charges against him.
Oedipus re-enters, and there is a rather tedious quarrel which
appears to have little significance, but of which the dramatic
effect is to show us Oedipus, who is not only hot-headed but also
obstinate, further stiffened in his attitude of disbelief, an attitude
therefore of something like impiety. Jocasta enters, and after the
quarrel has been more or less patched up, Creon goes out, and
Oedipus explains the scene to Jocasta, saying that Creon has
induced Teiresias to accuse him as the slayer. Jocasta tells him
that he need trouble nothing about that. The oracle long ago
declared that Laius was to be killed by his own son: whereas
he was actually killed by a party of robbers: so, she says,
oracles which have been wrong once are more than likely to be
wrong again, and Oedipus can neglect them. But she finds
Oedipus not reassured but troubled by her words, and asks the
reason. The damage has been done by a detail which she
introduced quite casually and naturally in her description of
the death of Laius, which has struck a chord of memory in
Oedipus. She happened to mention that Laius was killed where
three roads met, and a few inquiries make Oedipus morally
certain that he has been the slayer whom he has himself
denounced. He explains that he is son of Polybus, king of
Corinth, and his wife Merope, but when someone at a banquet

taunted him with being no son of Polybus, he went to Delphi and got no answer to his initial question, but was told that he was fated to kill his father and marry his mother. Fleeing from this doom he journeyed to Thebes, and on the way met an old man with attendants who treated him discourteously, and he had killed them all but one. If this old man was Laius he has cursed himself. The only hope is that the survivor will adhere to his tale that Laius was killed by a party of robbers. The hope is slender, but he must be summoned. Jocasta explains that as soon as the man returned, and found Oedipus reigning, he asked leave to return to his work in the distant pastures. Oedipus gives orders that he is to be summoned. This marks, as it were, the first climax of the play. And we are now expectantly watching to see how the knowledge of the greater horror will come to the doomed king. A chorus intervenes, on the usual moralizing theme of Greek tragedy, the arrogance that precedes a fall. Then there enters, not the herdsman, but a messenger from Corinth. And we wonder for a moment how he is going to advance the catastrophe. Polybus is dead, he says, and Oedipus is to be king of Corinth. Jocasta is triumphant at this proof of the falsity of the oracle. Oedipus when he hears the news shares her scepticism. But when Oedipus explains to the messenger that he still has fears about the part of the oracle which foretold that he should marry his mother, and says that for that reason he is afraid of returning to Corinth, the messenger, with the best intentions, to dispel his fears, tells him that he was no kin to Polybus, but that he, the old messenger himself, when a herdsman on Cithaeron years before, had received Oedipus as an infant from a herdsman of Laius': and the chorus interject that this second herdsman is probably the one whom Oedipus has just summoned. We watch with admiration the perfect simplicity and naturalness by which the final revelation is provoked. Jocasta makes a frantic attempt to avert the discovery. Oedipus can see nothing in her attitude but a reluctance to find that she has married beneath her, and his last words to her are bitter and scornful (it is the same hard truth to life that we see in the last words of Deirdre and Naisi[1]). Jocasta rushes into the palace with an ominous farewell. There follows a short and comparatively cheerful choric song. Then enters the herdsman

[1] In Synge's *Deirdre of the Sorrows*.

of Laius and the tension is strained to breaking point. In spite of the old man's efforts, Oedipus terrorizes him into speaking, and within a few lines the truth is clear to Oedipus and he rushes into the palace. There follows a choric ode of the ordinary moralizing kind. Enter a messenger to describe the death of Jocasta and Oedipus' blinding of himself. This vivid messenger's speech prepares us for the entrance of the blinded Oedipus. From this point the play moves quietly to its conclusion. The scene between the dignified and kindly Creon and the humbled Oedipus is a fine one: nor can anyone who has seen or read with imagination the scene when his two daughters are brought in to Oedipus ever again think of Sophocles as cold or lacking in humanity.

That is a bare outline of the plot of a great tragedy, and it is impossible within my limits of space to give any conception of the subtleties either of characterization or of language, in particular the play of dramatic irony. But even from so bare an outline you will realize the extreme skill with which the threads of the plot are interwoven and no superfluous detail is introduced. There is no character who is not essential, there is no attempt to diversify or complicate the action by the introduction of an underplot. The dramatist realizes that the story is all the more overwhelming and tragic from its bare simplicity, and he can trust his audience to agree with him. If you will compare the treatment of this Oedipus story by Sophocles with its treatment by later dramatists you will find clearly illustrated the peculiar qualities of Greek drama. For a full examination of the way in which the story is treated by Seneca, Corneille, Voltaire, and Dryden I must refer you to Jebb's introduction to his edition of the *Oedipus*. But the main point of difference, and the one that is relevant for our immediate comparison, is that none of the other four dramatists is willing to rely upon the simple plot as Sophocles gave it them; or perhaps they are distrustful of their own powers of handling it; but for whatever reason they all introduce some quite irrelevant love interest or under-plot, which no doubt diversifies the drama, but by diversifying distracts. Voltaire and Corneille would no doubt have repudiated with horror the suggestion that they were anything but 'Classic,' but the truth is that they are afraid of the pure unadorned classic severity.

I propose to say nothing of Senecan tragedy. The omission is, in one way, serious, but there are, I think, considerably more important things for us to consider, and since the influence of the Senecan upon the Elizabethan drama is a commonplace of all textbooks you can find it there. The influence is no doubt strong, and worth studying, but I will recommend to your consideration an admirable paper by A. D. Godley,[1] distinguished by all his scholarship and all his sanity, in which he suggests that the influence is less detailed than is often supposed and that the laborious search for verbal parallels may be an amusing recreation but is hardly serious literary criticism.

I propose in the rest of this chapter first to examine some attempts at the imitation of Greek drama in English, and secondly to compare and contrast the Elizabethan drama with the Greek.

Matthew Arnold, as might have been expected, set himself the task of writing a Greek drama in English: and the result was *Merope*. We are told by an editor whose enthusiasm got the better of his judgement that Arnold has 'produced a poem which is not only the nearest approach possible in any modern language to Sophoclean tragedy, but he has illustrated, as effectively as Sophocles himself could have done had he written in English, all that can be achieved in impression by dramatic art working under the conditions imposed on it by the Greeks. If Goethe's test of what is of real permanent value in poetry be the residuum left after the subduction of its accidents and of all that constitutes its sensuous charm, then in Merope we have a criterion of Greek tragedy. For what no modern poet can reproduce is the power and magic of the language and of the rhythm.'[2] That, surely, is near to nonsense. It means just this, that the English language is intrinsically inferior to Greek, which is more than doubtful, and that Matthew Arnold is as great a dramatist as Sophocles, which is untrue, and the falsity of which Arnold himself, to do him justice, would have been the first to assert. If *Merope* is indeed a criterion of Greek tragedy, then all that one can say is that the world for two thousand years has been strangely deluded, and that 'Securus

---

[1] In *English Literature and the Classics*, Oxford, Clarendon Press.

[2] Churton Collins, preface to edition of *Merope* and Sophocles' *Electra*.

iudicat orbis terrarum' is a sentiment with no foundation in
fact. The truth surely is that *Merope*, as one would expect from
so true and careful a scholar as its author, is an exact reproduc-
tion of the *form* of one type of Greek tragedy[1]; and as such it
merits careful study from anyone who, though ignorant of
Greek, wishes to gain some notion of what, in form, a Greek
tragedy was like. But it is not in the least true, as Churton
Collins seems to imply, that the only factors in drama with
which one need reckon are the form and the verse. There are
such things as dramatic imagination and intensity of emotion.
These are common to great drama whatever its form; it is the
lack of them which makes inferior drama in any form; and in
these qualities *Merope* is conspicuously lacking, Sophoclean
drama conspicuously rich. When once *Oedipus* has fastened its
grip upon the emotions there is no escape; one reads or watches
in thrall till the end. But *Merope* may at any moment slip from
the drowsy fingers, and the seeing of it on the stage is a thing
imagination boggles at. The characters in the one play are men
and women in whom their presenter is passionately interested,
however severely he curbs his passion. The figures in the other
are marionettes moving through a number of stereotyped
situations with a propriety which is equalled only by their
frigidity. The truth is that *Merope* is a perfect example of what
Greek tragedy is often *supposed* to be, 'silver-grey, placid and
perfect,' and for that very reason has no resemblance of any
kind whatever to what a Greek tragedy actually was, of all
creations of the human imagination one of the most profoundly
moving and unsparingly poignant.

Far nearer to a Greek tragedy, at least in certain essential
qualities, is a work which it is the fashion to describe, whether
for praise or blame, as hopelessly un-Greek, Swinburne's
Atalanta. There is, I think, a certain amount of confusion
of thought about this. Because Swinburne was in the main a

---

[1] The type which Aristotle considered only the 'second-best',
though he admits that it is sometimes ranked first, owing to the
'weakness' of the spectators; it is the type which has 'an opposite
issue for the good and bad characters', and *Merope* is not a tragedy
at all in our sense of the word, any more than Euripides' *Ion* is, or a
tragedy-comedy of Beaumont and Fletcher, since, though tragedy
has been imminent, it is averted, and the outcome is a 'happy-ever-
after' one.

very typical 'Romantic' it seems to be assumed that he was incapable of writing anything 'Classic.' And it is of course true that many things in *Atalanta*, and many of the loveliest things, are totally unlike anything you will find in Greek tragedy. The chorus on spring, for example, is one of the loveliest pieces of melody in any literature, but it is not Greek. The descriptions are often too highly coloured and, what is worse, long-winded, with the characteristically Swinburnean, but singularly un-Greek, fault of a superabundance of unnecessary epithets. And there is sometimes a facileness of sentiment which again is as far from the Greek temper as anything well could be. But, as against all this, the form is Greek; the stichomythia is often as brilliantly concise and finished as anything in Euripides; the characters, though they take too long to say them, say the Greek and not the English things; there is often a fine restraint and simplicity of expression; and, above all, there is real feeling and fire. I submit two short passages; and I want to ask any readers who are familiar with Greek tragedy to dismiss from their minds all presuppositions about Swinburne being an incurable Romantic (remembering if they like, that he was at any rate a respectable Greek scholar) and just listen to the words, and, as they listen, ask themselves whether these lines, if put into Greek, might not come straight from a Greek tragedy, not only because of the perfect simplicity and adequacy of the expression, but also because of the very nature of the thought so expressed. The first is from the final κόμμος[1], the second is the end of Meleager's dying speech and Atalanta's two lines of reply. The first is, incidentally, one of the most perfectly cadenced pieces of melody that even Swinburne ever wrote.

MELEAGER

Would God ye could carry me
Forth of all these;
Heap sand and bury me
By the Chersonese
Where the thundering Bosphorus answers the thunder of
Pontic seas.

[1] An interchange between chorus and actors.

OENEUS

Dost thou mock at our praise
And the singing begun
And the men of strange days
Praising my son
In the folds of the hills of home, high places of Calydon?

MELEAGER

For the dead man no home is;
Ah, better to be
What the flower of the foam is
In fields of the sea,
That the sea-waves might be as my raiment, the gulf-
stream a garment for me.

CHORUS

Who shall seek thee and bring
And restore thee thy day,
When the dove dipt her wing
And the oars won their way
Where the narrowing Symplegades whitened the straits
of Propontis with spray.

And now the conclusion of the whole drama: Meleager, dying, speaks;

And now for God's sake kiss me once and twice
And let me go; for the night gathers me,
And in the night shall no man gather fruit.

ATALANTA

Hail thou: but I with heavy face and feet
Turn homeward and am gone out of thine eyes.

And now we come to the last, and by common consent the greatest, of our examples of imitations of Greek tragedy, the last work of its great author. There are those who see in *Samson Agonistes* the evidence of the flagging of Milton's powers, who think it the work of a tired man. Well, if he was tired, he had good cause to be so, and it is perhaps enough to transfer to him the words of 'Longinus' on Homer and the Odyssey: 'If I speak of old age, it is nevertheless the old age of Homer.' But there are others who see in *Samson Agonistes*, and I think rightly, the consummation of Milton's art. There is perhaps no work in English which gives so vividly the impression of being the work of a man who was entirely sure of his artistic competence. There are more 'wonderful' works, works of clearer 'genius,' where the beauties seem to be the outcome of the divine accident which we call inspiration; and of Milton's own work *Paradise Lost* has greater splendour. But as an example of the best kind of 'conscious' art, in which the artist knowingly means every thing he says, and says exactly what he means, no more and no less, *Samson Agonistes* stands alone. And for this last work of his life, in which he was to find the divinest pleasure of the creator who knows that he cannot bungle his creation, Milton chose an imitation of Greek tragedy. We may regret that for his imitation Milton should have chosen this particular type of Greek tragedy, when there were other and finer types waiting for presentation in English; but, granted the choice, the result is as nearly perfect as any such transference can be. The form is an exact copy of an early type of Greek tragedy of which the *Prometheus Vinctus* of Aeschylus is the greatest example that we have. In this there is, in the ordinary sense, no plot, but rather a succession of scenes which exhibit the leading character in conversation with a series of other characters and with the chorus. The chorus too is used in the earlier Greek manner as an integral part of the action, indeed as an actor, not merely as a commentator upon the action, though it serves that purpose as well. The result is of course that attention is throughout centred upon the main character, and the other characters are no more than so many mirrors to reflect light upon him from different angles. And this result suited both Milton's aim and Milton's temperament better than a more intricate design; since there can be no reasonable doubt that Milton was attracted to the story of Samson by its similarity to his own, and that he was throughout seeing himself as Samson, and speaking though Samson's lips. And Milton, though the least vain of men, was one of the most egotistical; and, if he was to take the stage at all, he must hold it throughout. So, though making his drama less fit for the stage (for which he says it was never intended), he secured the extreme simplicity of impression of such a play as *Prometheus*. And since, through Samson, he can express the whole power of his own strongly passionate nature, as he looks back at the varied history of his own life, he secures also that intensity of emotional impression without which his drama would fail to remind us of the Greek. It is perhaps worth noticing that we find in *Samson* a note that we can, I think, find nowhere else in Milton. We have had the lightness of *L'Allegro*, the forceful compression of the sonnets, the strong splendours of *Paradise Lost*, but here for the first time we meet with a quality hitherto the least Miltonic of all, a certain gentleness, the resignation of which so many Greek choruses are full. Here is a passage, which (particularly the two last lines) makes us ask ourselves whether we have not moved from the temper of Satan to the temper of *Oedipus at Colonus*.

> All otherwise to me my thoughts portend,
> That these dark orbs no more shall treat with light,
> Nor the other light of life continue long,
> But yield to double darkness nigh at hand:
> So much I feel my genial spirits droop,
> My hopes all flat, Nature within me seems
> In all her functions weary of herself;
> My race of glory run, and race of shame,
> And I shall shortly be with them that rest.[1]

Finally, what of the chorus? Milton was perhaps the most skilful technical artist who ever handled the English language, and the choruses of Samson are certainly his most brilliant technical *tour de force*. They give, as nothing else in English, that impression of infinitely varied flexibility without loss of form which is the mark of the Greek tragic chorus. They are the

---

[1] *Samson Agonistes*, 590–8. I wonder how many readers will agree with me in finding here a curious similarity in 'tone' to a most unexpected poet, W. B. Yeats:

> 'Tell them who walk upon the floor of peace
> That I would die and go to her I love;
> The years like great black oxen tread the world,
> And God the herdsman goads them on behind,
> And I am broken by their passing feet.'
>   (*The Countess Cathleen*, closing lines).

true English *vers libre*, and modern versifiers would do well to study them. Milton earlier discarded rime and now in the end he discards recurrent metre. But it is just because he has passed through a long discipline in both rime and metre that he can discard them without his freedom becoming licence. The whole difference between Milton's choruses and so much modern 'free verse' is that they *are* verse. That is, they are perpetually suggesting a particular rhythm, but before that rhythm is fully established another is suggested. The effect is the counterpart in rhythm of *terza rima* in rime. I submit for examination a semi-chorus near the end of the play. Without going into minor details, will you just notice the swinging dactylic rhythm of the second line, re-echoed rather hesitatingly in the fourth after the strongly marked iambics of the third, which themselves prepare the way for the solemn beat of the description of the living Dread. Then look at the slow movement, as the destruction is importuned, and the hurrying hawk-like swoop of its descent; and finally, at the end, the startling effect, after the suggestion of the smooth opening dactyls, of the staccato final monosyllable.

> While their hearts were jocund and sublime,
> Drunk with idolatry, drunk with wine,
> And fat regorg'd of bulls and goats,
> Chaunting their idol, and preferring
> Before our living Dread, who dwells
> In Silo his bright sanctuary:
> Among them he a spirit of phrenzy sent,
> Who hurt their minds,
> And urg'd them on with mad desire
> To call in haste for their destroyer;
> They only set on sport and play
> Unweetingly importun'd
> Their own destruction to come speedy upon them.
> So fond are mortal men
> Fall'n into wrath divine,
> As their own ruin on themselves to invite,
> Insensate left, or to sense reprobate,
> And with blindness internal struck.[1]

[1] *Samson Agonistes*, 1669–86.

With *Samson Agonistes* we may leave the English imitations of Greek drama and turn to our own native product. And we are at once conscious that we are dealing with something not only wholly un-Greek, but also with something very peculiarly English. There is in the English temperament something which loves compromise, the combination of apparently incompatible elements in a whole, which, as we characteristically say, 'works,' And this temperament finds its expression no less in the English drama than in the English constitution. The very last thing the typically English drama aims at is an unbroken harmony of emotional impression: it loves discords, which may or may not be resolved. The English dramatist never says 'this is a tragedy, so we must be grave throughout,' or 'this is a comedy, so gravity must be avoided like the plague.' He says 'this is a play, for presentation on the stage, before an audience of Englishmen; it is a case of "As they like it" and "What they will"; and if they like a strange combination, that is their look out and not mine; and for that matter I like it too.' And this tendency appears throughout English drama. In the Elizabethans the mixture is often crude, high tragedy and broad farce coming, as it were, in successive slabs. In later drama the changes of tone are more continual and more delicate. But the same instinct is always at work. One of our most perfect, and perfectly artificial, comedies has at one point, if only for half a minute, all the force of tragedy. If anyone does not feel the sudden tension as the screen falls, and the note of 'Chaos is come again,' in Sir Peter's 'Lady Teazle, by all that's damnable,' he is not, I think, feeling the crisis as Sheridan felt it. Shaw, as an introduction to one of the most deliciously comic scenes in English, puts into Caesar's mouth one of the most superb pieces of English oratory. *The Lady's not for Burning* is a shot silk of comedy and something much graver. If you want another instance, go away back before the Elizabethans and read *Troilus and Criseyde*. Tragedy? Yes. Comedy? Yes. But, rather than either tragedy or comedy, Life. That is the point. To the English writer life, as he knows it, and as he sees his fellows living it, is more important than art. It is no doubt possible to isolate the tragic elements in life and make an artistic creation of them, or to isolate the comic elements and make a similar creation of them; and no doubt also by taking the two creations in turn it is possible to arrive at a composite picture which is a true enough picture of life. But neither creation is by itself true. And this way of going to work seems to the English writer to depend on a series of false abstractions. He prefers, even at the sacrifice of artistic unity of impression, to cut his section clean through, and see all the elements at once. He knows that, even if a king has been treacherously murdered, there will be a porter to open the gate, that he will probably be half-drunk and certainly amusing. He knows that even if a king's son has returned to avenge his father's death and meet his own, that will not prevent his meeting such ordinary persons as gravediggers, and that, being what he is, a great gentleman, he will meet both death and gravediggers with equal security and poise. He knows that a girl at whose birth a star danced, who seems to live for nothing but the polishing of the starriest and keenest-cutting diamonds of wit, may without warning tell her lover to kill his best friend; and that events which seem hurrying straight for tragedy may suddenly, with a change of wind, find themselves precariously beating up for harbour. And knowing all this he is going to put his knowledge on the stage, secure that his audience, who know it too, care more for the play than for the pigeon-hole of the category in which they are to put it.

It is the same instinct which makes the typical English dramatist, from Shakespeare downwards, impatient of 'the unities.' He is interested in writing an effective play and he is quite clear that the way to do it is not to pin up in front of him a card of rules imported from across the Channel. It may easily happen that his plot is one which is made more effective by limitation in place and time: if so, he will write a play which will 'conform to the unities.' But it was not with any idea of consciously conforming to the unities that he so wrote it. He wrote it because that was the way to handle that particular plot; and he will go on to another play which flagrantly outrages all the unities, and again it will be with no academic notion of running a tilt against a theory he dislikes. He is much too busy with his drama to be worried about theories; all he knows is that here is a plot which has to be handled quite differently from the former plot if it is to be effective. Here, in the unities, is one of the great differences, perhaps the greatest difference, between the Greek drama and our own. For, though it is a fallacy that Aristotle laid down the unities as rules, it is, as we have seen, a fact that Greek drama did, as a matter of practice, indeed of necessity, conform to them, And the result is a limitation of range, since only certain plots can be effectively presented with these restrictions, and only a parti-cular kind of dramatic effect can be produced. It is worth while spending a little time in considering this point, and it is possible to illustrate it without going to Greece, since our own literature provides a hackneyed but still illuminating example of the same plot being treated by two writers, one conforming to the unities and the other disregarding them. If you look at the story of Antony and Cleopatra you will see that it consists in bare outline of nothing more than a series of oscillations on the part of Antony. He is like a compass needle, swinging this way and that under the influence of various attractions; loyalty to his wife (comparatively weak), loyalty to Rome (stronger), loyalty to his soldiers and the joy of feeling their loyalty to him and his own powers as a great leader in battle (by far the strongest), but after each oscillation turning again to what for him is the magnetic and irresistible North, Cleopatra. Now it is clear that this is not *in itself* a dramatic subject, since there is no forward movement, but only movement about a fixed point; nor is it in itself even a great subject for any treatment, dramatic or otherwise, since the depiction of a man dominated by passion to the exclusion of other loyalties is apt to be tedious or even sordid. But the subject may become great and moving if the main figures are of sufficient stature. If we are aware that the man who is dominated by passion is a great figure in the world, and that consequently his subjugation is a critical event in history, and his fall something that has affected the lives of men from then till now, then the whole spectacle takes on a deeper significance. 'You shall see in him,' says Philo of Antony at the opening of Shakespeare's play, 'the triple pillar of the world transformed into a strumpet's fool.' Unless we can be made to realize that this man *is* the triple pillar of the world it matters very little whether he is transformed into a strumpet's fool or into anything else; but if he is the triple pillar of the world and we realize it, we are aware that his transformation will shake the world. Further, and from the purely dramatic point of view

this is important, the greater Antony is, the greater by implication is the woman who can so subdue him, and, moving further
round the same circle, the greater *she* is, the less ignoble does *his*
passion become. So that in both ways the drama is rescued from
the danger of becoming either trivial or sordid. But I suggest
that this enforcement of the realization of Antony as a great
historic figure cannot be performed by any dramatist, however,
skilful, within the limits of the unities. You must have space to
do it in, you must be able to set your characters moving against
the background of the whole civilized world. It is inadequate to
tell the audience that Antony has been from Alexandria to
Rome to meet Octavius; you must be able to *show* him at
Rome, settling the fate of the world, and then at Alexandria
again, in the toils. You must be able to take your audience to
the tumult of the battle that decided the fate of Europe, and
thence back to the Monument. All this can only be done if you
are willing to disregard entirely the unities of place and time.
And the more completely you disregard them the more spacious
can you make your play. It may be a mistake to select that
particular story at all for dramatic treatment, but if you select it
that is the only way in which it can be made great. If you insist
both upon selecting that story and also upon observing the
unities you doom yourself to failure from the start. This Dryden
found. He wrote a play which from the technical point of view
is as nearly perfect as may be; it has some admirable versifica-
tion, and at least one fine scene; it is excellently constructed and
neatly rounded off. But it is hard to believe that the same story
is being related. All the grandeur has gone, and most of the
passion. We are never in the smallest danger of being swept off
our feet. We are watching two individuals, a man and a woman,
neither of them particularly remarkable, whose fate is of no
particular importance to anyone but themselves. And the drama
is saved from being sordid by becoming trivial. Each play might
well have have had the title of the other, Shakespeare's being indeed about the World lost (well or ill) for Love, and Dryden's just
about a man and a woman, Antony and Cleopatra. This is not a
criticism of Dryden's dramatic skill—he failed where no one
could have hoped to succeed, and he probably came nearer to
success than any other dramatist could have come—but it is a
criticism of his judgement in choosing this of all Shakespeare's

plays for treatment under the restrictions of the unities. And
his failure illustrates the point that some stories can be treated
under the unities and others cannot. Some again can be treated
in either way, though the effect will be different. Imagine that
Dryden had selected *Macbeth* rather than *Antony and Cleopatra*
for his experiment. The play will begin with the fifth scene of
the first act of our present play (Lady Macbeth reading the
letter) and will then move forward on much the same lines to
an accelerated dénouement. The general result will be a marked
increase in simplicity and in speed, a marked increase therefore
in intensity. It is this intensity which is perhaps the clearest
distinction between Greek drama and ours. Most readers are
aware that the effect of *Othello* is unlike that of any other great
Shakespearean tragedy. And if you examine wherein this
difference consists, you will find, I think, this: that it consists in
whereas in other plays there are periods of relaxation, when
the progress of the main action is slowed up, and sometimes
indeed almost ceases, in *Othello* the progress is never intermitted,
but proceeds with a steady and relentless acceleration to the
tragic climax. And, in consequence, our feelings are kept under
a strain which is not only continuous but steadily increasing.
And I suggest that, if you regard the first Act as a prologue,
the rest of the play does pretty closely conform to the unities.
The place is Cyprus; the time thirty-six hours; the unity of
action almost complete. If you wish to illustrate this point to
yourselves further, may I suggest a comparison of *The Winter's
Tale* with *The Tempest*? The one has an arrogantly cavalier disregard of the unities, and the other closely conforms to them.
Would you not agree that the impression of the one is an impression of diffusion, of the other an impression of intensity, or,
if that word seems inappropriate to a non-tragic play, of concentration? Suppose the two plays to have been tragedies—as
one of them might easily have been—and one knows that *The
Tempest* would have 'felt' like *Othello*, and *The Winter's Tale*, for
all its similarity of subject, would not.

After examining certain salient points of difference between
the dramas of Elizabethan England and of Athens it may be
worth while to spend a short time looking at one or two
unexpected resemblances. We need not spend time over such
things as the use in both of dramatic irony, since that is an

obvious part of the stock-in-trade of any reasonably skilful dramatist; though it is perhaps worth mentioning it, if only for the reason that so much is said about it in reference to the Greeks, as though it were their peculiar prerogative, that we are sometimes in danger of forgetting that Shakespeare in his use of it is second to Sophocles alone, if second to him, and is certainly superior to the other two great Athenians. Nor need we labour the point of the resemblance on the one hand between the diction of Aeschylus and that of Shakespeare in his more bombastic and grandiloquent flights, and on the other between the diction of Euripides and that of some of the later Elizabethans, notably Ford. Those resemblances have to do partly with periods in the development of the respective dramas and partly with merely temperamental differences between writers. But two points are worth notice, Shakespeare's use of a 'choric' equivalent, and the conclusions of his tragedies.

Now in one sense, of course, the plays of Shakespeare have no chorus, except the merely clumsy animated stage direction who comes on, for example, in *Henry V*. But if we approach the question in a less mechanical way, not by asking whether there is a *dramatis persona* called 'Chorus,' but by asking whether in a Shakespearean play we are apt to find a person or persons who perform the function of the chorus in a Greek play, we shall find that the answer is 'Yes'. The Greek chorus do three things; they provide a musical interlude, a relaxation, the only relaxation, of the tragic tension; they comment dispassionately upon the action, or at least much more dispassionately than the actors; and they are part of the ordinary life of the world, the frame in which the tragic picture is enclosed, or, if you like, the background of ordinary affairs against which the tragic action is set. Now I think we shall find that these functions of the Greek chorus are performed in Shakespeare, but not by anything called a chorus, a thing obviously artificial, and artificial in a frigid way which was peculiarly abhorrent to Shakespeare and his audience; they are divided between two classes of people, first the clowns and fools, and secondly a class of characters of whom Shakespeare is particularly fond, the plain honest men, the people like Horatio and Kent. We have no time to deal at length with the clowns and fools, fascinating study though they are, but even a cursory examination seems to show this: that they do for the most part provide relief, not by any means always a relief which in any proper sense of the word can be called 'comic,' but a relief by a change of emotion, which may be tinged with comedy. The porter in *Macbeth* is no doubt, and was meant to be, a comic figure, but he performs, I think, a curious double function; he interrupts the tragic progress, and so relieves the tension; but by removing us for one moment from the actual whirling stream of the tragedy, and setting us as it were, on the bank, he gives us a chance of appreciating with increased, not diminished, vividness its implacable power. He also represents the ordinary every-day life of men; De Quincey's point is a true one, for all that he wearies one and almost makes one suspect its truth by his characteristically laborious over-emphasis. The porter's business in life is to open gates, and whoever he is to admit and to whatever scene of blood and horror he is unwittingly admitting them, he is going to carry on this business. And in the process he makes some entertainingly philosophic comments. The grave-diggers in *Hamlet* have much the same dramatic value. They are amusing, they show Hamlet in a peculiarly delightful light before the final catastrophe, their business in life is to dig graves and it matters nothing to them who the tenants of their houses are, and they too can philosophize about life and death in the light of their profession. The fool in *Othello* is negligible. In *Antony and Cleopatra* the clown with the figs is from one point of view nothing but a skilful dramatic device for heightening the suspense. We know that as soon as he has taken himself off the stage Cleopatra can get on with her dying, and we are as impatient with him as she is; for we know that we are waiting for one of the supreme moments in all poetic drama. But we are also, though less consciously, aware of something more. As the clown goes out, back to his ordinary life, we catch a mental glimpse of the bustle of the great city at its work and play, and it is from that glimpse that we turn to watch the queen, arraying herself for the last of her lovers. The fool in *Lear* is of course the greatest of all. And he is peculiarly interesting because of the kind of relief which he provides. No one, not even the most bigoted supporter of the exclusively '*comic* relief' theory, is going seriously to maintain that the fool in *Lear* is in any sense a 'comic' figure. In a tragedy so overwhelming and titanic an essentially comic element would indeed be tastelessly incongruous. But nevertheless the fool does provide a sorely needed relief for our battered emotions. He does it by translating us from the realm of the tragic to that of the pathetic; and pathos is, if one may use the word, 'easier' than tragedy. It makes less stringent demands upon us, and is less exhausting. But here again, as with the porter, the temporary relief enhances the total effect of the tragedy. It gives time, as it were, for a partial healing of the torn emotions, so that they are ready for the next onset of the eagle of tragedy.[1]

The other part of the choric functions is, in *Lear*, performed by Kent. His business is to be the faithful friend and adviser, loyal and sane. He is one of the grains of the salt of the earth who keeps the whole wholesome. His obvious counterpart in *Hamlet* is Horatio, but, in that play, part at least of the function of the chorus is in the hands of Fortinbras. It is he who makes the comment that we are waiting for at the end of the play. 'He was likely, had he been put on, to have proved most royal.' And the counterpart of these two characters in *Othello* is at first sight an odd one. It is surely Emilia. She represents the sanity of the ordinary world going about its ordinary avocations; like Juliet's nurse, she is plain and blunt, uncomprehending and coarse, but she is part of the staple of life and not one of its exceptions. And at the end, caring nothing for Othello's position, and knowing little of her husband's plots and Othello's agonies, she makes the straightforward comment that we have longed but hardly dared to make, 'O gull, O fool, as ignorant as dirt.'

The truth is that Shakespeare produces all the effects of the Greek chorus, but more tellingly because less obtrusively, and because the effects were dictated to him not by tradition, or by an artistic canon, but by his sense of the truth of things. He knew, what Stevenson later in so many words expressed: 'The shadows and the generations, the shrill doctors and the plangent wars, go by into ultimate silence and emptiness;

---

[1] It may be noticed that the Fool, no less than porter, grave-digger, and old man with figs, is carrying on his ordinary avocation, but, because the avocation of King's Jester is not familiar to us, we are apt to miss the fact.

but underneath all this, a man may see, out of the Belvedere
windows, much green and peaceful landscape; many firelit
parlours; good people laughing, drinking, and making love as
they did before the Flood or the French Revolution; and the
old shepherd telling his tale under the hawthorn.'[1]

And, lastly, for Shakespeare's final curtains. I wonder whether
it has ever struck you with surprise that the conclusion of a
Shakespearean play is not at all what you would expect the
conclusion of an Elizabethan play to be, that it is quieter, that
there is an odd absence of the 'strong' curtain, that ridiculous
dramatic abomination whereby, when the reunited lovers are
clasped in a passionate embrace, or a man is lying stabbed and
turning a white face to the limelight, a bell rings and the figures
are hidden, till in a few minutes the rapturous lovers or the
corpse are bowing and smirking to the audience. But absurd
though it is in its results (which are not indeed an essential part
of it) this strong curtain does end the play at its climax, on its
top note of emotion. And the Elizabethans being what they
were, with their love of the startling and the violent, one would
have said *a priori* that there was certain in their drama to be a
preponderance of strong curtains. Whereas there is no such
thing. And if one asks why, the answer is very simple. There was
no curtain to be strong. The conclusion of the Elizabethan play
is one of the most interesting examples of the effect of stage
conditions upon dramatic technique. The Elizabethans in a
tragedy liked plenty of corpses. Very good, by all means let us
have them. But what are we to do with our corpse-strewn stage
at the end? Even the Elizabethan audience, though it could
stand a good deal, could hardly put up with a general resurrec-
tion and perambulatory exit. If by a wise parsimony in murder
you can get your corpses on to a curtainable bed then you can
cover 'the tragic lodging of this bed' and the survivors can go
off to a council. But otherwise there is nothing for it but some
kind of stretcher-bearer procession, which has the additional
advantage that it gets all the characters, living or dead,
decorously off the stage. The same thing, you observe, happens
in comedy, which is also apt to end with a procession, though

---

[1] Stevenson, 'An Apology for Idlers', And cf. Hardy 'In Time of
the "Breaking of Nations".'

to altar rather than to grave. It is this necessity for clearing the stage which leads, for example, to the unhappy series of mésalliances, 'put on by cunning and forc'd cause', with which *Measure for Measure* closes. But, whatever the cause, the outcome of all this is that the climax of an Elizabethan play must by some distance precede the actual conclusion. In other words we are going to end on a quiet note, in a manner very similar to that of Greek tragedy. And the Elizabethan dramatists cheerfully accepted the compulsions of their stage and made their limitations seem pure gain. There is not only a rounded completeness of artistic impression, but a sense also of truth to life, created by the conclusions of *Hamlet* or *Othello* or *Antony and Cleopatra*, which no abruptly strong curtain could give. Anyone will vividly realize this who has ever had the misfortune to see a modern actor-manager playing tricks with Hamlet. I saw one such vandal who rang down the curtain at the obvious point, 'The rest is silence.' I leave you to imagine what the play lost. All I want to do now is to remind you of the conclusions of the great tragedies, and ask you to notice how in one at least there is the general philosophic comment so characteristic of Greek tragedy, how in three of them there is a kind of epitaph on an individual, but how in all of them the broken threads of affairs are knotted so that ordinary life can proceed. It is characteristic of a nation which has the Roman instinct for society as more important than the fate of the individual, however great. The king's government must be carried on.

MACBETH

Malcolm . . . this, and what needful else
          That calls upon us, by the grace of Grace
          We will perform in measure, time, and place:
          So, thanks to all at once, and to each one,
          Whom we invite to see us crown'd at Scone.

KING LEAR

Kent The wonder is he hath endur'd so long:
      He but usurp'd his life.

Alb. Bear them from hence. Our present business
Is general woe. (*To Kent and Edgar*) Friends of my
    soul, you twain
Rule in this realm, and the gor'd state sustain.

Kent I have a journey, sir, shortly to go;
My master calls me, I must not say no.

Alb. The weight of this sad time we must obey;
Speak what we feel, not what we ought to say.
The oldest have borne most: we that are young
Shall never see so much, nor live so long.

OTHELLO

Cas. This did I fear, but thought he had no weapon,
For he was great of heart.

Lod. (*to Iago*)   O Spartan dog,
More fell than anguish, hunger, or the sea,
Look on the tragic lodging of this bed;
This is thy work, the object poisons sight,
Let it be hid: Gratiano, keep the house,
And seize upon the fortunes of the Moor,
For they succeed to you. To you, lord governor,
Remains the censure of this hellish villain,
The time, the place, the torture: O, enforce it!
Myself will straight aboard, and to the state
This heavy act with heavy heart relate.

ANTONY AND CLEOPATRA

Caes.   she looks like sleep,
As she would catch another Antony
In her strong toil of grace.

.   .   .

Take up her bed,
And bear her women from the monument;
She shall be buried by her Antony.
No grave upon the earth shall clip in it
A pair so famous: high events as these
Strike those that make them; and their story is

No less in pity than his glory which
Brought them to be lamented. Our army shall
In solemn show attend this funeral,
And then to Rome. Come, Dolabella, see
High order, in this great solemnity.

HAMLET

Ham. The potent poison quite o'er-crows my spirit:
I cannot live to hear the news from England,
But I do prophesy the election lights
On Fortinbras: he has my dying voice;
So tell him, with the occurrents, more and less,
Which have solicited. The rest is silence. (*Dies*)

Hor. Now cracks a noble heart. Good night, sweet prince,
And flights of angels sing thee to thy rest! (*March within*)
Why does the drum come hither?

Enter Fortinbras, and the English Ambassadors, with drum, colours and Attendants.

Fort. Where is this sight?

Hor.   What is it you would see?
If aught of woe or wonder, cease your search.

.   .   .

And let me speak to the yet unknowing world
How these things came about:

.   .   .

Fort.   Let us haste to hear it,
And call the noblest to the audience.
For me, with sorrow I embrace my fortune:
I have some rights of memory in this kingdom,
Which now to claim my vantage doth invite me.

Hor. Of that I shall have also cause to speak,
And from his mouth whose voice will draw on more:

.   .   .

Fort.   Let four captains
Bear Hamlet like a soldier to the stage,
For he was likely, had he been put on,

To have prov'd most royal: and, for his passage,
The soldiers' music and the rite of war
Speak loudly for him.
Take up the bodies: such a sight as this
Becomes the field, but here shows much amiss.
Go, bid the soldiers shoot.
(*A dead march. Exeunt, bearing off the bodies; after which
a peal of ordnance is shot off.*)

✢✢✢✢✢✢✢

'CLASSIC' AND 'ROMANTIC'

'HEAVEN SAVE US!' SAYS THE DESPONDENT READER, 'THE OLD Tweedledum and Tweedledee again.' I want to suggest that the two terms become Tweedledum and Tweedledee only if by slack thinking we allow them to become so, and that in fact they represent a real and significant distinction.

Literary discussions, and the pages of textbooks, are full of labels and accepted clichés, and it is a salutary exercise from time to time to pull ourselves up with a round turn and ask ourselves what precisely we mean by them. If the writer or speaker has himself no very precise notion of what he means, the reader or audience is not likely to derive much illumination; the idea communicated will be at best vague and at worst positively misleading. Take for example 'picaresque'—how seldom that word is rightly applied; yet it has a quite specific, and narrowly specific, meaning. Or 'nostalgic,' which presents an equally specific metaphor, and does not mean just 'sentimental' or 'moving' or 'wistful.' Or—a modern favourite— 'evocative'; evocative of what? it is merely slovenly to use it as meaning nothing more precise than 'stimulating the emotions.' Or look at some well-worn labels, much favoured by the more pedestrian literary historian. 'The Scottish Chaucerians'—as a purely chronological label, to designate briefly Henryson, Dunbar, and some others, it is perhaps a legitimate convenience, but it has dangerously misleading implications, first that the poets are like one another, which Henryson and Dunbar

manifestly are not, and second that they are primarily imitative
poets though they happen to be Scottish. Or 'Restoration
Comedy'—where the trouble is the other way round, since it
may be a convenient label for a *type* of play, but is somewhere near
nonsense as an indication of *date*; of the famous plays which we
naturally think of under that label only Wycherley's are even
approximately 'Restoration', and the rest are a minimum of
seven years post-the-1688-*Revolution*.

Now of all these labels and clichés two of the most frequently
bandied about are 'classic' and 'romantic,' and one of them
is universally used as part of the description of a particular
and important 'period,' while the other is affixed as an
accepted label to a number of writers who seem, on examination, to exhibit differences almost as strongly marked as
their resemblances. It seems, therefore, in the interests of
any precise critical thinking, desirable to examine whether
the distinction between them is a real one, and, if so, what
exactly it is.

I am prompted to make yet one more attempt at the examination, to hash over yet again the many times cooked cabbage,
by the re-reading of a brilliant, but I think misleading, lecture
delivered by that versatile man of letters who, after 25 years of
the writing of some excellently spirited fiction and the compiling
of some admirable anthologies, held for thirty distinguished
years the King Edward VII chair of English Literature at
Cambridge. Sir Arthur Quiller-Couch was not a 'scholar' in the
narrower, or perhaps in any, sense, nor did he produce any
critical magnum opus. But if it is any test of a Professor, in his
capacity of teacher, that he can hold very variegated audiences,
and can, in men and women whose academic disciplines lie in
fields far different from his own, kindle an ardent enthusiasm
for the noblest things in letters, and so enrich their equipment
for life, Q was a great Professor. But he was also, I think, a much
more considerable critic than it is at present the fashion to admit.
His reputation has suffered for various reasons. In the first place,
he believed in the spoken rather than the written word as the
proper medium for teaching—it was, after all, the only medium
for the great teachers of the older days before printing, and they
were probably the greater teachers for the limitation. If Q
could later reach a wider audience from the printed page, well

and good; but the lecture came first. I doubt whether he ever gave a perfunctory lecture, composed in haste and delivered with half his mind while the other half was straying back to his desk and the paragraph left lying unfinished on it. He realized that a lecture is as much a literary form as an essay, but a different form, so that an essay written to be perused in the study may be a first-rate essay but, if read aloud to an audience, will never be anything but a third-rate lecture. So he put the best of himself into his lectures and took great pains to make them as effective as he knew how, *as lectures*; and it was still as lectures that they appeared in print, so that we never lose the sense of being a member of an audience under the persuasion of a speaker. As a result he is described as the after-dinner-speaker among professors. That phrase is intended as derogatory, but at least it admits that he is always eminently and refreshingly readable. Why not? To be an illuminating critic it is not necessary to be unreadably dull.

Even more fatal has been his rich humour, because there is a sadly large body of serious readers who hold as a curious article of faith that if a writer has something of serious importance to convey he must be pompously solemn in the conveyance; that you cannot be at once serious and entertaining. Writers as diverse as Shaw and Coward and A. P. Herbert have all tripped over this stumbling block, been written off as jokers when they were most in earnest, laughed at instead of attended to.

It is true that ease of manner may sometimes disguise importance of matter, that the chuckle at the felicitous turn of phrase with which a point is made may momentarily distract us from the urgency of the point itself. But it is our own fault if we allow that to happen. And I think that any reader who will accept Q's method, and who is not repelled by generous enthusiasm for the great things or, on occasion, unsparing exposure of the trivial and mean, will find that for genuine insight, the power of penetrating through accidents to essentials, Q has few rivals among English critics, and even fewer as an exponent, implicitly always, explicitly sometimes, of the belief that literature is only a part of life, is of value only as it helps men to live their lives—a belief without which all criticism is sterile.

I have spent a page or two on Q partly for the pleasure of
paying a small tribute to work which I read, and re-read, with
ever-increasing illumination and refreshment, but also because
I want to make clear that my disagreement with a particular
lecture does not arise from an antecedent general under-rating
of the writer. The lecture is entitled 'On the terms "Classical"
and "Romantic," and it appears in the first volume of
Studies in Literature. I earlier described it as brilliant; and
so it is. But it is brilliance of a poor kind, a bit of special
pleading. Q., by a confusion of thought, is decoyed into
an attack on his advertised subject by his vigorous dislike of
his real subject; and so he is trying hard to score his bulls on
the wrong target—and scores little better than outers even on
that. None the less, even special pleading, if the advocate is
able enough, is a stimulating challenge, forcing one to re-
examine one's own assumptions.

Q opens fire by commenting on the frequent use of the two
words in handbooks to literature, usually with the implication
that the qualities which they purport to describe are opposite
if not mutually exclusive. He then suggests that many of his
audience have no very sharply defined idea of how, why, or
how far, they are opposite or exclusive. Black and white (say
black print on white paper) are easily distinguishable, and can
be precisely delimited. But 'we cannot draw any such line
between "classical" and "romantic" work; since, to begin with,
the difference between them is notional and vague (even if we
admit a true difference, which at this point I do not).' It begins
to be clear along what lines and towards what conclusion the
argument is to move. The difference is 'notional,' certainly; so
are many other differences, not only in the field of literature—
truth and falsehood are presumably 'notional.' But Q is trying
to edge us in the direction of accepting an equation of 'notional'
with 'vague.' He then cites three passages, one from *Hamlet*, one
from *Lycidas*, one from *The Cenci*, challenges us to say of each
whether it is 'classical' or 'romantic,' and suggests that we may
be 'inclined to temporise', even perhaps 'admitting that, all
things considered, there was a little bit of both about them.' One
observes that he tacitly excludes the other possible answer that
they are neither, nor even a combination of the two. There may
be extensive tracts of literature which are independent, owing

allegiance to neither 'classical' nor 'romantic,' nor even governed by a condominium.

There follows a polemic against the use of abstract terms such as 'classicism' and 'romanticism.' And the section ends with this sentence 'Shakespeare, Milton, Shelley did not write "classicism" or "romanticism." They wrote *Hamlet, Lycidas, The Cenci.*' Readily granted, and a salutary counterblast against the vague use of abstract verbiage. But it is not the end of the matter. Praxiteles sculptured his famous Hermes, and an unknown sculptor the Aphrodite of Melos; they did not sculpture the classical style. But those two statues have something in common, of which the most untrained eye is aware, which makes them akin to one another, and alien in both technique and appeal from the work of, say, Rodin or Epstein. And there is no reason why, if we keep our heads, we should not try to find terms, even abstract terms, and use them to express that kinship and that difference, instead of denying that the kinship and the difference exist.

The polemic against the misuse of abstract terms in criticism is abundantly justified; but it is largely irrelevant, and the special pleading and the confusion of thought become yet more clearly apparent. Q hopes that if he can sufficiently discredit the 'classical-romantic' contrast he can coax us into accepting some such process of thought (it can hardly be called a syllogism) as this: 'many abstract terms are used in criticism; "classicism" and "romanticism" are such terms; they purport to describe a contrast which does not exist, and are therefore meaningless and valueless; therefore all such abstract terms are meaningless and valueless.' Or, alternatively, 'many abstract terms are used in criticism which have no relation to reality because what they purport to describe does not exist; "classicism" and "romanticism" are abstract terms; therefore the contrast between "classical" and "romantic" does not exist.' Neither argument of course is put as baldly as that, and both are elegantly packaged for the consumer, but not even Q can persuade one to accept so palindromic an affair, in which premise and conclusion are interchangeable.

So from this point onwards Q reverts to the subject first announced and concentrates on discrediting the terms 'classical' and 'romantic.' Two points are worth keeping in mind while

examining his argument, first, that the discrediting is so important to him for other purposes that his survey of the problem is
from the outset prejudiced, and second—and much more
important—that the fact that a term can be, and often is,
loosely used or misused has nothing whatever to do with its
intrinsic validity. A pound note is not worth less than £1
because it is in the hands of a dishonest rogue. Similarly, even a
proof that two terms are improperly used to describe a hypo-
thetical contrast goes no way at all towards proving that the
contrast itself is illusory. But that is precisely what Q is trying
to do.

His method is to pose a number of rhetorical questions, in
which he puts into our mouths a series of demands which we
may be supposed to make. As thus: 'Do you postulate, for
romantic writing, glamour and magic, adventures on "perilous
seas in faery lands forlorn?" Very well; then I exhibit this same
Odyssey to you, with its isle of Circe,

> where that Aeaean isle forgets the main,

its garden-court of Phaeacia, its wonderlands of the Cyclops,
the Sirens, the Lotus-eaters, its scene, a moment ago related, of
the princess playing at ball with her maidens on the strand; or I
exhibit the marvellous tale of *Cupid and Psyche*, parent of a
hundred fairy-tales dispersed throughout the world (*Beauty and
the Beast* for one).

'Or is it passion you demand of romance? I exhibit [Q, like
the elder Brother, "is taken with a short fit of"— Matthew
Arnold] the passionate verses of Sappho . . . beginning

> φαίνεταί μοι κῆνος ἴσος θεοῖσιν
> ἔμμεν ὤνηρ . . .

or a speech of Phaedra, or Catullus' lyric of Acme and Septimius.

'Is it pathos?—utter pathos? I exhibit to you Priam on his
knees, kissing the hand that has murdered his son; Helen on the
wall; Andromache bidding farewell to her husband at the gate,
her boy kicking and crowing on her arm at sight of his father's

nodding plume; and again that last glimpse Virgil gives of her, in slavery, returning from vows paid to the dead—of her that was "Hectoris Andromache."

'Is it any sense of predestinate doom fulfilled? I refer you to the last stand of the Sicilian expedition in Thucydides. Or is it a general sense of the woe, the tears, the frailty, the transience inherent in all human things? A dozen passages from Virgil might be quoted.'

That is an appeal by a brilliant counsel to the emotions of a jury, but it is no more. It is hard to know where to begin on it. Take the first point, adventures and glamour; there is a tacit assumption, bolstered up by a suggested similarity in temper between two lines—of which the second is not by Homer but by Andrew Lang—that because the *Odyssey* has adventure it *ipso facto* has 'glamour.' But one of the most obvious points in any discussion of 'classic' and 'romantic' is that strange adventures can be treated in two different spirits, one matter of fact, one 'glamorous.' And what in the world is there of either glamour or magic in the description of Nausicaa washing the clothes and playing ball?

'Or is it passion you demand of romance?' That is not a question that can be answered by a monosyllable. No one 'demands' a continuous spate of passion in either 'classic' or 'romantic' writing. Passion may be in place in one kind of poem and out of place in another kind, whether classic or romantic. It may turn out that the essential difference lies not in the presence or absence of passion, but in the restraint or lack of restraint with which the passion is expressed. In this section Q seems to be putting up an Aunt Sally so tottering that it is hardly worth the trouble of knocking down. He makes the assumption that the people who are so stupid as to think that there is a real difference between classic and romantic are making that difference coincident with a difference in date, so that they take all the Greeks and Romans to be 'classic.' But almost every reader will willingly admit that much of Catullus is not in the least what he means by 'classic.' Oddly enough, Q himself seems to fall into this chronological error, since he says later, of a nineteenth-century poem which he regards as both classical and romantic, 'It is as classical as anything in Catullus.'

'Is it pathos?' One notices in passing that the lecturer does not seem to know Homer very well, since Astyanax—in Homer's account at any rate—so far from kicking and crowing at the sight of his father's plume, is scared stiff by it, and shrinks back crying into the arms of his nurse, not of his mother. It is a small point, no doubt, but it does not promote confidence, since it is a product of that unscholarliness of the imagination which is so much less venial than verbal errors. Nor is it clear that Helen on the wall is presented as a pathetic figure, except perhaps at the moment when she fails to see her brothers. Otherwise she is almost a favoured daughter of Priam, and wins from the old men their famous tribute. However, two of the episodes, Priam with Achilles and Andromache with Hector, are profoundly pathetic and most movingly presented. But one may still suggest that there are different ways of handling pathos, as there are of passion.

'Is it any sense of predestinate doom fulfilled?' What perversely mischievous imp tempted Q to add this question to his others? Is any reader in the least likely to make any such demand from romantic writing or to find it satisfied if he does? He would be much more likely to demand, and find, a picture of man as master of his fate than as the victim of a predetermined doom. And why, having asked a foolish question, does Q cite such an inapposite reference? To begin with, there *was* no last stand. In the battle in the Great Harbour the Athenians were desperately attacking, trying to break out, not to repel; and the last bloody butchery on the banks of the Assinarus of the remnants of the army, worn out by nine days of harassed retreat, and now pitifully grovelling for water, was hardly a 'stand.' Nor is the disaster presented to us as any sort of fulfilment of predestinate doom, or as anything but the result of political ineptitude at home and military folly in the field; also perhaps as an example of νέμεσις—but that is a different thing from 'predestinate doom'.

All this specious special pleading leads up to the following astonishing conclusion: 'I think, if you will look into "classicism" and "romanticism" for yourselves, with your own open eyes, you will find—though the whole pother about their difference amounts to nothing that need trouble a healthy man—it amounts to this: some men have naturally a sense of form stronger than their sense of colour: some men have a sense of colour stronger than their sense of form.'

On this two comments may be made. First, even if we admit that the difference can be expressed in terms of form and colour, or of any other two single and specific qualities, we need not be thereby appreciably nearer to admitting that the difference is illusory or trivial. Suppose that one takes two substances and prepares a number of specimens containing varying proportions of the two. At the two ends of the scale will be specimens containing 99 per cent of x and 1 per cent of y, and 1 per cent of x and 99 per cent of y. And those specimens will be markedly and recognizably different from one another (suppose that $x=$ whisky and $y=$water). But in the middle of the scale will be a number of specimens not at all so easy to distinguish. (These correspond roughly to the dubious examples which we were challenged to assign to one class or the other.) But the difficulty of discrimination in this middle range does not make the difference between the ends of the scale any less wide or less easily perceptible. In other words difference of degree may become so great that it becomes difference in kind.

Second, the view that the whole difference can be reduced to degrees of keenness in sense of form and sense of colour is not borne out by the facts. It is surely obvious that the *Ode to a Nightingale* was written with a sense of form as keen as that which controlled the writing of an ode of Horace. It was a *different* sense of form, no doubt, but just as sensitive. The real difference, I think, is a difference of spirit, of attitude not only towards literature but towards life. That difference Q either does not recognize, or, for the purpose of his argument, neglects. But if it exists, as I hope to show it does, it is a far more essential difference than that between form and colour; and it has nothing at all to do with dates or countries; it has to do with the spirit of the particular writer.

Q ends his lecture as follows: 'I advise that it may help our minds to earn an honest living if we dismiss the terms "classical" and "romantic" out of our vocabulary for a while.' By all means let us dismiss the *terms*—if we can find better ones to replace them. But let us by no means be diverted, either by this advice or by the covert sarcasm implied in 'a healthy man' earlier, from an honest attempt to discover whether a difference exists which those terms have commonly been used to denote, and to determine whether, if it exists, it is important enough to justify a considerable deal of 'pother.'

In the long progress of literature, which began with the first letter and the stranger's mud-filled hair, and to which only the angel of the last trumpet will call a halt (nor even he, if Kipling's heaven is true), there seems to be observable an oscillation, a recurrence of cycles like those of the old philosophers, over which opposed spirits ruled. The spirits' names were Love and Strife, causing in turn order and dissension. In literature there seem to be two spirits which produce somewhat similar results, though they go by less plain designations, and do not work with such cyclical regularity. Or, to put it in another way, through the texture of the great web to the weaving of which all writers in all ages have in their degree set their hands, run some threads of gold, sometimes appearing very plainly, sometimes almost wholly hidden under more violent colour, but reappearing with the added effect of the return of a motif in music. And these threads are used mainly for designs of severely beautiful simplicity. The quiet Greek border and the rare flowers which relieved it, at the end of the weaving long ago rolled off, were golden. Later, in our own literature, the threads were almost submerged in a great riot of full-blooded colour and flamboyant design, and when next they come to the surface there is a great deal of tinsel about which obscures them. Still later, in the weaving yet on the loom, there are, among many pieces of strange beauty both in form and colour, at least two pieces of grave and severe design which again are golden.

To leave the vague realms of metaphor, the difference between the 'classical' and the 'romantic' is, I think, a difference both of spirit and of form: primarily one of spirit, only secondarily and by consequence one of form. May we, as a preliminary to investigation, dismiss from our minds all question of the two terms 'classical' and 'romantic,' dismiss even any question of literature, and transfer our attention to another art, architecture; and then examine not two books but two buildings, Westminster Abbey and the Parthenon? Take the Parthenon first. The first impression which it makes upon one is, I suppose,

that of a magnificent simplicity. It is—or, strictly, it appears to
be—a harmony entirely of straight lines. It relies for its effect
not at all on surprise: when you have seen one of the great
pillars you have seen them all: and when you look at the building from any of its four angles, you have as complete a view as
the limited human vision can have of any enclosed rectangular
building: and you know that, except for the sculptures of
the metopes and pediments, the two unseen sides are exactly
similar to the two sides which you have seen. Nor does the
building rely upon any feeling of mystery: it stands four-square
in hard, bright light; its effect is a mass effect; no detail is of
importance in itself (again perhaps excluding the sculpture):
you are not asked to admire a particular bit of fluting,
you are to admire the Parthenon. The result is a building
of a superb and completely satisfying adequacy. Before we
leave it, may I suggest one question, of which the relevance
will appear later? As you look at the Parthenon, how does
your eye move?

Now let us come to Westminster Abbey: or if that building
is too full of the voices of the past and the shades of the great
dead for any of our nation to look at it dispassionately, then
take any other great Gothic building, Chartres if you like. The
first impression is of a magnificent complexity: it is an intricate
harmony of straight lines and interlacing curves. It relies very
largely upon an element of surprise: as you turn the corner of a
transept you feel not certainty but expectant surmise: a yard's
change of position will give you an entirely new vista of different
pillars and vaultings. It relies largely upon a sense of mystery,
or at least of vagueness: there are all manner of half tones,
lights and shades, and dim recesses: the details are in a sense
subordinate to the total effect, but the total effect is one of
incomparable richness from the variety of the details, and most
of the details are worth individual study, whether it be the
elaborate tracery of a window, or a gargoyle, or the different
carving of two different bosses. Nor do I think that anyone
would naturally describe the total effect as one of adequacy or
satisfiedness: it induces a certain restlessness, since you know
that as you let your eye rove, or as you wander round the
building, you will come upon new beauties: and in a sense it is
not complete. I do not mean that it *demands* further treatment:

but you feel that it would permit it. And now may we revert to
the question 'how does one's eye move in looking at the
Parthenon?' Is it not true that it moves mainly on horizontal
lines, between which the vertical lines are links, and that at no
point does it stop, not even at the top angle of the pediment,
but is gently led down again so that it never wants to stray
outside the confines of the building. But if you ask the same
question with regard to a Gothic building, is not the exact
converse true? Your eye is moving perpetually upon vertical
lines between which the horizontal lines of clerestory and so on
are links: and when your eye has been led up to the culmination
of a piece of vaulting it does not naturally come down the groin-
ing of the other side: it comes back to the floor and starts again,
and, if I may put it so, when it reaches the top it wants to go
through the roof. Take an even stronger instance: what
happens when your eye has run up Salisbury Spire? Does it
come quietly home to earth again?

Now if anyone denies that those two buildings are the expression of fundamentally different ideals, and indeed of fundamentally different attitudes towards life; and says that the
difference amounts to no more than this, that one designer had
a keener sense of symmetry and the other of decoration, there
is no more to be said, to him at any rate. He will equally
refuse to see similar differences in other spheres. But anyone who
admits the difference in architecture will be ready at least to
consider the possibility of an analogous difference in literature.
There have been many attempts at defining the difference. Let
us begin with two. A distinguished professor of Humanity at
Edinburgh, W. R. Hardie, suggested that in classical art there
is always a certain acquiescence, whereas in romantic art there
is an element of discontent or aspiration. Walter Pater said that
romantic art has always a love of the strange whereas classical
art is a perfection of manner in treating of an authorized
subject. I think that the first observation shows much deeper
insight than the second. Pater's, indeed, is partly erroneous and
partly superficial. It is superficial in so far as it stresses technique
and not spirit, and erroneous in that it implies that the distinction is between an imperfection and a perfection of manner:
whereas, as I hope to show, the distinction on the technical side
is between two different manners, each in its kind perfect or

imperfect in proportion to the greatness or inferiority of the particular artist. I shall try to demonstrate the differences between the two spirits and the two techniques by a number of illustrations; and I suggest that in examining them it will be useful to keep in mind the architectural parallel and see how far it holds. (And I shall use the stock terms, 'classic' and 'romantic' as time-savers, to avoid such phrases as 'the one spirit which might be called the Parthenon spirit.')

In Greek literature most critics would concur in selecting Homer and Sophocles as the most 'classic' writers. There is no mystery about Homer: in spite of Quiller-Couch there is no 'glamour' in the magical sense. Indeed it is when he seems to be most dangerously skirting the reefs of the island of romance that he is most securely classic. When, for example, the flesh of the oxen of the sun bellows on the spits,[1] Odysseus and his crew consider indeed that it is somewhat untoward and cer- tainly ominous: they are properly impressed and sail on their way: but evidently the thing, like Michael Finsbury's lunch, might have happened to anyone. Consider for a moment the grisly picture which, say, Coleridge would have made of this scene. But with Homer even his horrors are in the sunlight. Also they are clear-cut. Take now three lines of *Christabel*:

> I guess, 'twas frightful there to see
> A lady so richly clad as she—
> Beautiful exceedingly!

How would a classic writer have phrased that? He would, surely, have omitted the first two words, would have said simply δεινὸν ἦν, and would by the mere omission have altered the whole tone of the passage, would have got the focus clear instead of deliberately blurred.

You will find in both Homer and Sophocles, and for that matter in Thucydides, the most rigorous restraint. Whether the episode is tragic, or horrible, or pathetic, it is, if anything, under-stated and left to produce its own effect. It is never stressed, never embroidered. There is a great deal of misunder- standing about the phrase 'the restraint of emotion.' It is sometimes used as though it meant an absence of emotion, but

---

[1] *Odyssey*, xii, 395–6.

the phrase as it stands is correct: you cannot restrain something which is not there to restrain. And the whole essence of this kind of restraint, the thing which gives it its peculiar and often overwhelming power, is just that the emotion is strong and even passionate, but is being ruthlessly controlled, ridden on the most savage of curbs. Look at that moment in the *Oedipus Tyrannus* when Jocasta sees that the disclosure of the horrible truth is inevitable and passes into the palace to kill herself. And this is what she says to Oedipus as she goes:

> ἰοὺ ἰού, δύστηνε· τοῦτο γάρ σ' ἔχω
> μόνον προσειπεῖν, ἄλλο δ' οὔποθ' ὕστερον [1]

or that other moment when Oedipus at last sees the truth himself, the moment which is, I suppose, the actual climax of the whole drama, when the emotions are at their highest tension. And in his agony of mind he speaks the simplest and most collected prose:

> ἰοὺ ἰού· τὰ πάντ' ἂν ἐξήκοι σαφῆ.
> ὦ φῶς, τελευταῖόν σε προσβλέψαιμι νῦν,
> ὅστις πέφασμαι φύς τ' ἀφ' ὧν οὐ χρῆν, ξὺν οἷς τ'
> οὐ χρῆν ὁμιλῶν, οὕς τέ μ' οὐκ ἔδει κτανών. [2]

We may compare this with the incoherent ravings of Othello. Is anyone going to say that Othello's anguish is deeper than that of Oedipus? I think not: nor, I am sure, has anyone the

---

[1] *Oedipus Tyrannus*, 1071, 2. 'Alas, alas, unhappy man. That is the only word I can speak to you, who will never speak to you again.'

[2] *Oedipus Tyrannus*, 1182–5. 'Woe, woe! All, as needs must, has become plain. O light, now may I look on you for the last time, seeing that I stand revealed as born to sin, in sin wedded, and a father-killer.' (The idiom of the first line is barely reproducible in English, and the deadly, and somewhat elliptical, plainness of the last two lines, not, I think, reproducible at all without absurdity. They are, literally, 'sprung from those from whom it was sin to be sprung' (i.e. not in itself but because of the sins that were to result), 'living with those with whom it was sin to live' (i.e. not only Jocasta, but also his sister-daughters), 'and having killed those whom I ought not.') I have laboured the point, in admitting defeat, because I know few more striking examples of the sometimes excruciating power of the ψιλὸς λόγος, the 'bare word,' in Greek.

right to say that either way of expressing emotion is more legitimate or more moving than the other. But they are not the same. Similarly, as has been well said, you cannot squeeze a tear from the pages of Thucydides, though he is narrating a tragedy and that tragedy his country's.

In Sophocles and in Homer—it is worth remembering that Sophocles is described as the most Homeric of the dramatists—you find that 'noble acquiescence' which is taken by some, rightly I think, as a mark of the classic spirit. I discussed this acquiescence earlier with regard to Homer, and need not cover the ground again.[1] In the *Oedipus Tyrannus* there is no hint of rebellion against the judgement of the gods for bringing down so frightful a doom on Oedipus, no suggestion that, where the sinner had sinned unwittingly, so disproportionate a punishment was a travesty of justice. There are the facts: he killed his father and married his mother: there is no more to be said ('They hired the money, didn't they?'). And the *Oedipus Coloneus* lays to rest any doubts that the *Oedipus Tyrannus* may have raised. Even in the *Antigone*, though there is a problem, it is a straightforward *practical* problem of conduct—ought obedience to the gods to override obedience to the state?—and not a problem of speculation, like those which harassed Aeschylus and Euripides. It is worth noticing, as disposing of the notion that the classical spirit is a matter of chronology, that here are two writers, belonging to the same age and country as Sophocles, who are in many ways far more different from Sophocles than is, for example, Landor. Aeschylus has something of the Hebraic fervour, the smouldering fire and the vast but sometimes cloudy imaginative power of the great Jewish prophets, qualities which are about the least Hellenic in the world, while Euripides is often frankly a rebel and always a sceptical inquirer.

And in Sophocles you find in its perfection what on the technical side is the hall-mark of the classic temper, a love of simple form and the absolute subordination of every detail to the mass effect. Let me repeat, at the risk of being wearisome, that the difference is not one between comparative *degrees* of perfection: it is a difference between *kinds* of perfection. In a work of a different type—and it does not follow that because it

[1] *See* p. 44.

is not 'classic' it is therefore 'romantic'—the details, though they contribute to the whole, are also memorable and important in themselves: but that is not the classic ideal. Is not the effect of the *Oedipus Tyrannus* just that of the Parthenon, a perfect harmony and balance and symmetry, a piece of absolutely satisfying work, complete within its own limits, and a work of which you have difficulty in isolating in memory any one detail? It is, as nearly as any human work can be, flawless. And then look at a work which is indeed not the most profound, nor the greatest, work of its great maker, but is by the common consent of critics, who all use the same word, his most 'wonderful,' *Antony and Cleopatra*. I need not elaborate the contrast: everyone is aware of the peculiar impression of that work, of a structural complication, but a strong emotional unity, in which the details often stand out vividly. I do not mean by that that *Antony and Cleopatra* is necessarily to be called romantic, though most people would so describe it. It is quite as absurd to suppose that because a thing is not classic it is therefore romantic, as to suppose that because a thing is not white it is therefore black: it may be red or green, but it is equally distinct from white.

Take one or two more instances. I said earlier that Johnson's famous translation of Callimachus' epitaph on Heraclitus is as false as it is beautiful: false, that is, to the spirit of the original. But here I need not try to ram down anyone's throat my own opinions of the difference between the two spirits, but can let two classical scholars speak for me. Here is Johnson's version:

> They told me, Heraclitus, they told me you were dead,
> They brought me bitter news to hear and bitter tears to
> shed.
> I wept as I remember'd how often you and I
> Had tired the sun with talking and sent him down the
> sky.
> And now that thou art lying, my dear old Carian guest,
> A handful of grey ashes, long, long ago at rest,
> Still are thy pleasant voices, thy nightingales, awake;
> For Death, he taketh all away, but them he cannot
> take.

Walter Headlam says of this:[1] 'That version, as I well know, is familiar and dear to many, and it is with great reluctance therefore that I am going to find fault with it; I should have little wish in any case to find fault with the author of *Ionica*: but if one is to appreciate the flavour of Callimachus, I must feel that this version does not represent it. The characteristic of Callimachus is reserve, even to excess; and this poem, as I read it, is the restrained, suppressed emotion of a man in mature life. Now Johnson's version has nothing in it of restraint; on the contrary it is, if anything, effuse in sentiment: the original in fact, is a *vin sec* and Johnson has turned it into sweet. Callimachus, I think, has given us something rarer and stronger and more deeply felt.'

The other great scholar whom I am calling in evidence is A. W. Verrall, criticizing Gilbert Murray's translation of the *Bacchants* of Euripides. 'His (Euripides') manner, so far, in the prologue, is animated and not undignified. But it is neither sublime, nor mystical, nor, in any sense of the word, religious. It is a plain style of narrative, having about as little elevation as is compatible with the form of poetry. It could not satisfy, and was not (one would suppose) designed to satisfy, as the style for a god, those who had seen gods presented by Aeschylus and Sophocles. And we observe that it does not satisfy Professor Murray. Mr Murray's prologue is not only more highly coloured, more poetical, but it has, what Euripides will not give, the note of sublimity and mystery.

> *Behold God's son is come into this land*
> Of Thebes, even I, Dionysus, whom the brand
> Of heaven's hot splendour *lit to life*, when she
> Who bore me, Cadmus' daughter Semelê,
> Died here.

This is a fine opening, and religious. This, or something like it, is what would have been put in the mouth of the Man-God by an Aeschylus or a Pindar. But let it be compared with the original. Can we suppose that the Διὸς παῖς (the son of Zeus) of Euripides, or the ἥκω (I have come) (a common form

---

[1] *Book of Greek Verse*, p. 303. His own translation is given above, p. 88.

of his theatrical prologists) had ever for any ear the arresting sound, as of some awful Revelation, which the translator strikes in *Behold, God's Son is come*? And if Euripides wished to suggest that the speaker is a superhuman, incomprehensible Being, in whom earth and heaven are united, could he not find, as our English poet can, language fit for the purpose, and say that, by the stroke of lightning, He, the Babe of Semele, was "lit to life"? What Euripides said is simply that the lightning "delivered" the mother. And as the two compositions begin, so each proceeds to the end. The prologist of Euripides concludes his narrative by saying twice, in plain terms, that his outward appearance, for the present, is merely human: *For this cause I have taken mortal form and changed my shape into the nature of man.* From the English alembic this emerges thus:

> For this I *veil my godhead* with the *wan*
> Form of the things that die, and walk as man.

This is, or might be, the language of godhead veiled. But in Euripides there is neither veil to see through nor deity to see.'[1]

Now after all this I may be very rightly challenged to give my own definition of classic and romantic: and with the pistol at my head and 'stand and deliver!' in my ears, the best I can do is this. The 'classic' temper is one which accepts the inevitable and does not wear itself out in attempts to solve the insoluble; it feels emotion strongly, but expresses it with equally strong restraint: it dislikes the mysterious: in technique it insists upon harmony, the subordination of details to the whole, and upon simplicity. The romantic temper questions and rebels: it feels emotion strongly and expresses it with little restraint; it has often a vivid love of the mysterious; and in technique it insists equally upon perfection of form, but it permits, and even prompts, greater elaboration and richness, and at least condones the concentration of attention upon details. But after all these elaborate phrases I come back to my original illustration. The Parthenon is one thing, and Gothic architecture is another.

How do the two tempers appear in our own literature? Chaucer will not fit into any pigeon-hole. 'God's plenty'

[1] *The Bacchants of Euripides.*

cannot be parcelled up into attitudes and tempers. So far as he has an 'attitude to life' at all it is one of eager perception of all the varied experience that life has to offer, of tears or joy, and he has a rich, all-embracing humour which does not seem to be an essential element in either the classical or the romantic temper. The Elizabethans again refuse to be categorized. They are too exuberant to be classical, yet life to them is exciting, as it was to Odysseus, rather than mysterious or wonderful. They have much of the classical writers' undazzled clarity of vision, but they are often extravagant in the expression of it. Yet, on occasion, though they do not even aim at the Sophoclean perfect subordination of parts to whole, you find in them the Sophoclean restraint and simplicity of expression. And the quiet lines stand out in peculiarly vivid relief from the exuberance which surrounds them. Compare with the lines which I quoted from the *Oedipus*, not this time the ravings of Othello, but such things as

> 'I am in the way to study a long silence,'[1]

or

> Well, Juliet, I will lie with thee tonight,'[2]

or

> Unarm, Eros, the long day's task is done
> And we must sleep.[3]

or its echo

> Finish, good lady, the bright day is done,
> And we are for the dark.[4]

Or perhaps most Sophoclean of all, coming as it does at the culminating moment of a great tragedy,

> The rest is silence.

It seems, therefore, that, like Chaucer, the Elizabethans present neither temper, or both, as in a later century, and in less

---

[1] Webster, *The White Devil*, V. vi.
[2] *R. & J.* V. i. 34.
[3] *Antony and Cleopatra*, IV. xii. 35.
[4] *Ibid.* V. ii. 192.

vigorous contrast, did Matthew Arnold. But I submit that that
does not imply that the two tempers are not distinguishable.

In contrast to these gay adventurers, spreading their audacious
sails with such uncalculating zest, stands a grave lonely figure,
whom one is at first tempted to single out as the supreme
master of 'the classical' in our literature. But when one comes
to examine him, Milton turns out to be less easily 'assignable'
than one expected. If one takes his later work, especially
Samson Agonistes (and adds, from the earlier, the sonnet on his
blindness), hardly Sophocles surpassed him in finished artistry,
in perfection of subdued colouring, in subordination of means
to end, and in strength of feeling strongly restrained. But much
in the earlier work is thoroughly Elizabethan. And even in
Paradise Lost, though there is no relaxation of unrelenting
control, there is often a burning fervour (as there is also in the
Piedmont sonnet), a gorgeousness of colour, and a gem-
encrusted splendour, which go beyond the 'classical.' As a
result, an attempt to distinguish different elements in Milton is
uniquely illuminating if we are trying to delimit the 'classical.'
It seems to me that in a large part of his work we can find all
the qualities which we can 'demand for' classical writing, but
that there is also an overplus, which does not indeed run
counter to his classical temper, but amplifies it, raises it to a
higher power. And I suggest that part of this overplus is due
to a strong moral sense, which is no necessary element of either
'classic' or 'romantic,' and part to an innate love of magnificence.

But when we leave Shakespeare's barbaric and wanton riot
in gorgeousness (the methods of his prodigal genius are those of
a wonderful child with a box of bricks and tubes of oil paint)
and leave also Milton's calculated splendour and the forged
harmonies of his cadence, then we move into a different world.

Less than a generation after Milton's death the eighteenth
century opened. The so-called 'Augustan age' in English
literature, and the eighteenth century as a whole, have had
many hard things said about them, many of them unjustified;
and the man who indulges in a general denunciation of the
century writes himself down an ass as surely as the man who
does the same for the Victorians. The men of the eighteenth
century made a superlative success of life *on their own terms*. But

those terms included a restriction of boundaries. Their aim was 'security,' both social and emotional, and they considered that the aim could be attained by the application of good sense and reason, forgetting that the spirit of man cannot live by reason alone. There was, I suppose, more good sound sense talked in the eighteenth century than in any other century in our history. But there was also a great deal of uninspired writing, just because the writers had not the least wish to be inspired. A fine folly was a laughing-stock and enthusiasm an offence against good taste; and inspiration was dangerously near to enthusiasm. Above all they ran away from the emotion of wonder like the plague. Wonder is a disturbing emotion. And though the pool of Bethesda gained its healing properties only when the waters were 'troubled,' the slightest ripple on the placid surface was avoided, and the rewards were forgone.

The age is often held up, whether to admiration, or—often by those who dislike both the age and what they mistakenly take to be 'the classical'—to reprobation, as being the most perfect presentation in English of the classical temper. The judgement is, I think, seriously imperfect, but not wholly mistaken. The germs of the malady from which the age suffered are latent in the classical ideal with its insistence on perfection of form. This part—the less important part—of the ideal the eighteenth century whole-heartedly embraced, and as a result it is full of incomparable craftsmanship. Whether Pope had much to say that was worth saying, or much feeling beyond angry resentment to express, is a matter of dispute; but there is no dispute at all about his sheer mastery over his tools, unrivalled among English, or perhaps any other, writers; and Swift, with plenty worth saying to say, and a deeper and worthier, because less personal, anger to express, shows in his different medium an even more powerful though less consistent mastery. Now it is a mistake to refuse admiration to technical mastery, and an even more grievous error to undervalue it, so long as it is being pursued as a means to an end beyond itself. But too many of the eighteenth-century writers worship it as an end *in* itself. The fire in the true shrine is neglected, and on the twin false altars of form and good sense the deeper qualities of feeling and imagination are sacrificed; if the lines are polished, the sentiment irreproachable, and 'Nature' accurately presented, the poet's task is adequately performed. What more could any reasonable man want? A merely reasonable man perhaps nothing. But a full man may want both feeling and imagination. Feeling and imagination, however firmly restrained and controlled, are vital parts of the classical ideal, without which it degenerates into a sterile 'classicism,' where there is no restraint of feeling because there is no feeling to restrain, and no control of imagination because there is little or no imagination to control.

After the eighteenth century, with its clear excellences and even clearer limitations, and in spite of a few premonitory voices of rebellion, it is with something of a shock that we find ourselves in the very different, and much more confused, atmosphere of the period which is known to literary history as 'the Romantic Revival.' It is a remarkably unsatisfactory label. If one asks what it was a revival *of*—since, unless a thing has existed before, it cannot be revived, though it may be born—the best that Echo can return by way of an answer is a reiterated 'Romance,' and we are left just where we were, since all we are offered is a definition of a thing by itself, not *ignotum per ignotius*, but *ignotum per se*. 'The Romantic Revolt' is a trifle less unsatisfactory, since we do know what at least half the phrase means; there was a revolt and we see what it was against. But the best label, if we must have one, is probably Watts-Dunton's 'the renascence of wonder,' since most of the writers of the time have this in common, that they recaptured the lost faculty of wondering. But we are wiser to repress any desire for labels, and be content to examine a number of writers who lived at about the same time, trying to discover whether, in spite of manifold and manifest differences, they were moved by anything which can reasonably be called 'the spirit of the age.' And it soon becomes clear that there was such a spirit abroad, very different from that which governed the preceding age. It was a spirit which blew very much where it listed, and could hardly be said to 'govern' anyone, since its concern was not with reason but with feeling and imagination. And of all human faculties reason is the most constant as between one man and another, so that the rational processes of one man will differ from those of his neighbour only in proportion to the degree of intellectual power with which they are applied, whereas feeling and imagination are among those most peculiar to the individual, so that the reactions to a common stimulus, the response to the same spirit, will be very diverse as between man and man. Wordsworth differs widely from Shelley, and both of them from Keats; Byron is no more than superficially touched by the spirit, and remains at heart in the preceding age, while Keats is profoundly moved to the centre of his being, and Coleridge profoundly but more intermittently; Hazlitt, De Quincey, and Lamb are not in the least alike, but none of them surely could have written as he did in any other age. Differences of manifestation cannot obscure the one-ness of the informing spirit.

Can one make an attempt to define this spirit by examining the manifestations? There is little sign of acquiescence, but rather a restless hunger after beauty, even exotic beauty; there is a consciousness, sometimes uneasy, of the secret and Circean powers of Nature, sometimes excited, sometimes beatifically tranquil, but always tinged with wonder; there is an uneasy questioning of the ordering of this life that stains the white radiance of eternity. The spirit appears in different guises, sometimes a wild-eyed Maenad, leading her votaries through sunless forests of enchantment, sometimes a gay-eyed laughing nymph, persuading those who will follow her to wander off the highroad down by-roads full of the magic of spring. But it is the same spirit, questing, wandering, and wondering, quite different from the other spirit which moves with the grave, wise eyes of Athene soberly along the highway, with an uncompromising directness of aim.

But one can go on analysing, making statements, spinning metaphors, without clinching anything, except for oneself. Indeed I believe that in the end everyone has to arrive at his own solution to the two problems, first, 'are there two spirits, two attitudes towards life, which are sufficiently opposed for the opposition to be worth observing?' and second, 'where, if so, in literature or elsewhere, am I myself aware that the opposition is presented?' So that all that anyone who is trying to clarify his own mind, and quicken his own apprehension, can do for anyone else who is engaged on the same enterprise is, not to argue, but to suggest, to present for examination what seem to him relevant examples. And this I will do.

Take first *Kubla Khan*, to many readers the most perfect single expression in our literature of what is ordinarily called the romantic temper. It is an unmatched record of a dream, with all the coherent incoherence of a dream; and one may observe the vague impression of mystery which, in the first few lines, is created by the negative epithets. The caverns are 'measureless' and the sea 'sunless,' where the writer of a different temper would have used defining positives. And alongside that passage put

> that untravell'd world, whose margin fades
> For ever and for ever when I move.[1]

Now take the end of Landor's imaginary conversation between Hannibal and Marcellus. Marcellus is dying captive in the hands of his great enemy, and he learns that his son has escaped: and he says, 'He would have shared my fate—and has not. Gods of my country! beneficent throughout life to me, in death surpassingly beneficent, I render you, for the last time, thanks.' And take the famous passage from 'Aesop and Rhodope,'

> Laodameia died; Helen died; Leda, the beloved of Jupiter, went before. . . . There are no fields of amaranth on this side of the grave; there are no voices, O Rhodopê, that are not soon mute, however tuneful: there is no name, with whatever emphasis of passionate love repeated, of which the echo is not faint at last.

With which one may compare

> Beauty is but a flower
> Which wrinkles will devour;
> Brightness falls from the air;
> Queens have died young and fair;
> Dust hath clos'd Helen's eye;
> I am sick, I must die—
> *Lord, have mercy on us!*[2]

---

[1] Tennyson, *Ulysses.*
[2] Nashe, *Summer's Last Will and Testament;* O.B.E.V. 167.

Here are two short lyrics concerned with that grim ferryman that poets write of.

> Stand close around, ye Stygian set,
>   With Dirce in one boat conveyed!
> Or Charon, seeing, may forget
>   That he is old and she a shade.[1]

> Crossing alone the nighted ferry
>   With the one coin for fee,
> Whom, on the wharf of Lethe waiting,
>   Count you to find? Not me.
>
> The brisk fond lackey to fetch and carry,
>   The true, sick-hearted slave,
> Expect him not in the just city
>   And free land of the grave.[2]

The instancing of the second suggests a comment or two on Housman, who is indeed something of a touchstone in this inquiry. How many of his poems can be claimed as 'pure classical?' Almost all of them have high excellences of form, of balance, of telling concision and concentration; but are we not aware in many of them, especially after several readings, of a discordant note in the feeling, of a slackened restraint, sometimes even of something almost bogus in the sentiment, almost falsetto in the irony? Again and again it seems to me he misses his effect, by the narrowest of margins, but fatally, for in this type of writing the narrowest miss is much worse than a mile. And he fails, I think, because, great classical scholar though he was, there was something in the 'classic' temper which was not wholly congenial to him and against which he sometimes rebelled—or to the exacting demands of which he had not always the stamina to respond—with results most illuminating to the enquirer. Take for example 'To an Athlete Dying Young.'[3]

---

[1] Landor, *Dirce.*   [2] Housman, *More Poems*, XXIII.
[3] *A Shropshire Lad*, XIX.

It starts admirably, pointing with the utmost verbal adroitness
the ironic contrast of situations, and it goes near to maintaining
that level till the last stanza. And then

> And round that early-laurelled head
> Will flock to gaze the strengthless dead,
> And find unwithered on its curls
> The garland briefer than a girl's.

Now is that, in spite of a translation of a Homeric phrase,
'classical' at all; does it even escape being a trifle 'sentimental'?
Or take 'Is my team ploughing . . .'[1]

> 'Is my team ploughing,
>   That I was used to drive
> And hear the harness jingle
>   When I was man alive?'
>
> Ay, the horses trample,
>   The harness jingles now;
> No change though you lie under
>   The land you used to plough.
>
> 'Is football playing
>   Along the river shore,
> With lads to chase the leather,
>   Now I stand up no more?'
>
> Ay, the ball is flying,
>   The lads play heart and soul;
> The goal stands up, the keeper
>   Stands up to keep the goal.
>
> 'Is my girl happy,
>   That I thought hard to leave,
> And has she tired of weeping
>   As she lies down at eve?'

[1] *Ibid.* xxvii.

Ay, she lies down lightly,
  She lies not down to weep:
Your girl is well contented.
  Be still, my lad, and sleep.

'Is my friend hearty,
  Now I am thin and pine,
And has he found to sleep in
  A better bed than mine?'

Yes, lad, I lie easy,
  I lie as lads would choose;
I cheer a dead man's sweetheart,
  Never ask me whose.

Now many readers rate that poem very high; they point, justly, to the quiet precision with which in the earlier stanzas the tension is increased, to the unforced power of 'Be still, my lad, and sleep', as the living speaker tries to evade the now imminent crisis, and to what they feel to be the climax, the whip-lash, of the last line. 'Can anything,' they say, 'be more effective, more typical of the "classical" manner?' Well, yes, I should instance several other poems of Housman's own which are more effective, because more classical, and I should suggest that in this poem it is precisely the climax which spoils the effect, and that just because it is *non*-classical. Is it not too obviously contrived, too self-conscious? Above all, is it not redundant? The true climax, surely, is not the last line but the last line but one. All that needs saying has been said, and the rest had much better have been silence. Contrast with this the impact of the last line of Kipling's 'Heriot's Ford' (a poem not unlike Housman's in form) which has ten times the ironic culminating force.

But against these two set the 'Epitaph on an Army of Mercenaries.'[1] Here we find strong feeling strongly, even harshly, controlled; balanced symmetry of form, each point in the first stanza being taken up in the second; the sparest

[1] *Last Poems*, XXXVII.

economy of expression (there is neither adjective nor adverb except for the necessary 'mercenary'); and a stabbing climax—which, as a small point, a writer of a different temper would have marked by the dash before the last two words which Housman will not permit himself. After the lapse of more than forty years it is perhaps as well to recall the circumstances of its writing. It appeared on the anniversary of First Ypres, and was a rejoinder to the unwary disparagement, by the Kaiser, as an 'army of mercenaries,' of one of the finest bodies of fighting men that ever went into action.

> These, in the day when heaven was falling,
>   The hour when earth's foundations fled,
> Followed their mercenary calling
>   And took their wages and are dead.

> Their shoulders held the sky suspended;
>   They stood, and earth's foundations stay;
> What God abandoned, these defended,
>   And saved the sum of things for pay.

It is a kind of writing which has become more frequent in our modern literature as we have reacted against both the 'romantics' and the Victorians. You will find it, for example, not uncommonly in Kipling's work, especially in the 'Epitaphs' in *The Years Between*.

> On the first hour of my first day
>   In the front trench I fell.
> (Children in boxes at a play
>   Stand up to watch it well).

As a useful reminder that any particular poet does not always write in the same particular way, contrast Keats' 'To Autumn' with any other of his Odes. In form it is almost identical, but that is apt to prevent us from seeing that surely a very different spirit is here Keats' 'presider.' Here are no flights of the imagination, and tranquil observation replaces unrest. Where are the viewless wings of poesy, or Bacchus and his pards, or the sovran shrine of Melancholy, or the

mad pursuit and struggle to escape? In their place is a rich
and acquiescent peace, content with the mellowness of Earth
in autumn.

May I, in conclusion, try to illustrate the contrast which
I have been suggesting between two very different spirits
by the juxtaposition of two passages on death? The first is
by a modern master of melody and leader of revolt, the
other by a young scholar who had no gospel and no heresy to
preach, but was content to walk on Helicon with the austerer
Muses of Hellas.

> Death at last for all men is a harbour; yet they flee
>   from it,
>   Set sails to the storm-wind and again to sea;
> Yet for all their labour no whit further shall they be
>   from it,
>   Nor longer but wearier shall their life's work be.
>   And with anguish of travail until night
>   Shall they steer into shipwreck out of sight,
>   And with oars that break and shrouds that strain
>   Shall they drive whence no ship steers again.[1]

That breathes of despair and revolt against fate; and it has a
haunting beauty. Here are six lines which show that a modern
writer need not fall short of the old poets of Greece either in
noble and balanced tranquillity of the spirit or in exquisitely
simple perfection of the letter.

> ξεῖνε, καλὸν τὸ ζῆν καταγώγιόν ἐστιν ἁπᾶσιν,
>   νηπυτίους γὰρ ὅμως νυκτιπλανεῖς τε φιλεῖ,
> δῶρα χαριζόμενον φιλίας καὶ τερπνὸν ἔρωτα
>   καὶ πόνον εὔανδρον, φροντίδα τ᾽ οὐρανίαν·
> τρυχομένους δ᾽ ἤδη κοιμᾷ τὸν ἀκήρατον ὕπνον,
>   πέμπει δ᾽ ὥστε λαθεῖν οἰκάδ᾽ ἐληλυθότας.[2]

[1] Swinburne, *Erechtheus* (4th chorus).
[2] Kenneth Freeman: It is the epigram with which he won the
Browne Medal at Cambridge. It is quoted in the 'editor's statement' prefixed to Freeman's book *Schools of Hellas*. Freeman himself
translated the whole epigram, but his rendering of the first four
lines—which by the kindness of the Headmaster and Librarian of
Winchester College I have been able to see—is curiously inadequate, so that the editor wisely confined himself to the almost
perfect rendering of the last two, and I have given the rest in prose.

I tell you, passer-by, that life is a good inn for all men;
for it welcomes alike the simple and the night-wanderers,
and dowers them with gifts of friendship and joys of love,
and toil that makes men noble, and mind that lifts them
    to the stars.
Then, when I was aweary, last and best,
    They gave me dreamless rest,
And sent me on my way, that I might come
    Unknown, unknowing home.

INDEX

INDEX